Eternal WOMANHOOD

Divine Attributes of Christlike Women

Eternal WOMANHOOD

Divine Attributes of Christlike Women

RICHARD J. ALLEN

Covenant Communications, Inc.

Cover image: *Living Water* © Howard Lyon, courtesy Altus Fine Art. For print information visit www.
altusfineart.com or call 801-763-9788

Cover design copyright © 2015 by Covenant Communications, Inc.

Published by Covenant Communications, Inc.
American Fork, Utah

Printed in the United States of America
First Printing: March 2015

20 19 18 17 16 15   10 9 8 7 6 5 4 3 2 1

ISBN 978-1-62108-910-0

To my lovely wife, Carol Lynn, my friend and partner for eternity. I am deeply grateful for her loving example and helpful counsel during the preparation of this book about the blessings that the daughters of God bring into the lives of all of us. Her life is for me a wonderful manifestation of the qualities of eternal womanhood.

FOREWORD

ALL OF GOD'S CHILDREN ARE blessed by the influence of eternal womanhood. The devoted women who inspire us on our mortal journey—caring mothers, wives, daughters, sisters, aunts, nieces, grandmothers—assist the Lord in awakening within us the light of life, the hope of glory, and the faith in everlasting family relationships.

Often we see in our minds and remember in our hearts the moments where mothers or sisters or other women have acted in love to bless our lives. Holding a burning candle, a kindly hand reaches out and shares the glow with those seeking to be warmed with the blessings of light. Such is the elect calling of eternal womanhood: to be the source of heavenly illumination for all the sons and daughters of God.

Fingers of charity gently stroke the cheeks of the lonely, the discouraged, the fearful—and thus awaken renewed feelings of hope and courage in a shadowy world of tribulation and challenge. Eternal womanhood partakes of the glory of divine power as the source of vital blessings to all who journey along the pathway of life.

The consoling fragrance of a tender flower, rising as a testimony of the beauty of God's creation, soothes the soul with the aroma of emerging life. Eternal womanhood is the flower of vitality and the font of heartfelt energy.

Similarly, the delectable fruit of the earth's abundance reminds each partaker that the mercy of the Lord sustains our lives along the mortal pathway. That same mercy empowers the spirit of eternal womanhood to quench the thirst and relieve the hunger of all who seek the gospel of living waters and the bread of life. Each daughter is divinely appointed to be "the mother of all living" (Genesis 3:20; Moses 4:26)—whether through maternal sacrifice or loving nurture.

What do we hear echoing across the landscape of Zion? Anthems of praise, melodies of thanksgiving, choruses of glory! The voices of cheer from God's faithful daughters resound in harmony to confirm the eternal truths of the plan of salvation and exaltation.

Beyond the sounds, savor, scent, touch, and sunshine of womanly service is the spiritual joy that flows into our lives when the daughters of destiny bear witness of the reality of the Father and the Son through their words and acts of enduring compassion as confirmed to us by the whisperings of the Holy Ghost. Our thanks rise toward the heavens for the blessings of all those who manifest the glory of eternal womanhood in the cause of Zion and awaken our vision to the blessings of eternal glory and everlasting life.

In his vision of the spirit world, received on October 3, 1918, President Joseph F. Smith saw many of the prophets and leaders of the Lord in that realm serving with devotion to spread the truths of the gospel to the anxious spirits awaiting the coming resurrection:

> Among the great and mighty ones who were assembled in this vast congregation of the righteous were Father Adam, the Ancient of Days and father of all,
>
> And our glorious Mother Eve, with many of her faithful daughters who had lived through the ages and worshiped the true and living God. (D&C 138:38–39)

Can we not see in our own minds and remember in our own hearts the moments when such "faithful daughters" have blessed our lives by the decisions they have made?

This book is a testimony of the sublime qualities of eternal womanhood that awaken within us a better understanding of our divine potential as children of God. In support of this objective, we provide a collection of what we call "living scenes" from daughters of destiny down through the ages. Each scene is anchored in details from the scriptures and unfolded in a narrative designed to bring the applicable theme to life.

Each chapter provides a short commentary on a chosen theme, followed by a three-fold panorama of insight exemplified in the lives of the daughters of destiny: "One Moment In Eternity," concerning a prominent personality of timeless interest; "Sisterly Echoes," concerning a lesser-known but equally exemplary figure; and "A Modern Moment," concerning a figure in our time. Each chapter ends with a section inviting readers to ponder creative ways to apply the examples of eternal womanhood unfolded in the various narrative scenes. Questions and prompts are given to engage the mind in ways that help us enrich learning in family and group discussions, reach out to others in sharing the gospel, and do a little better each day by applying the Savior's counsel, "Come, follow me" (Luke 18:22).

The writer Goethe ended his dramatic poem *Faust* with a memorable line: "The eternal womanly draws us onward." I hope and pray that the material in this book will draw us onward to strengthen testimonies, enhance hope, magnify faith, and encourage thoughts and actions that will serve to increase joy and peace in the homes and families of Zion.

I offer my sincere thanks to the editors and designers at Covenant Communications for their leadership and guidance in making this book available for students and teachers of the gospel.

The Author

TABLE OF CONTENTS

CHAPTER ONE

Divine Majesty

And Mary said, My soul doth magnify the Lord, And my spirit hath rejoiced in God my Saviour. (Luke 1:46–47)

ALL THE SONS AND DAUGHTERS of God have the opportunity to apply the principle of magnification as part of their service in living and sharing the gospel. We aspire to make things better, to lift others up, and to "improve the shining moments" all around us (see *Hymns*, no. 226).

As used in the scriptures, the word *magnify* (from the Latin word *magnus* or "great") means to make greater, to make more splendid, or to reveal more fully the majesty or magnificence of something or someone. There are four kinds of magnifying evidenced in the gospel. First, there is the process of magnifying *an office or calling* by accepting it with humility and gratitude, soberness and devotion (as in Jacob 1:19). By doing so, we next magnify *the Lord* and enlarge His holy name before the world (as in Luke 1:46–47—quoted above—and 2 Nephi 25:13). This process results in magnifying *ourselves* through His blessings (as in Joshua 3:7), thus allowing us to magnify *the gospel message* so that the pathway to eternal life is illuminated (as in Isaiah 42:21). Choosing to magnify in these ways is a service of divine majesty and eternal magnificence.

> " Choosing to magnify in these ways is a service of divine majesty and eternal magnificence. "

The role of eternal womanhood is a manifestation of this kind of service, for the faithful daughters of Zion choose to reveal in gracious ways the presence of God's touch and mercy in our lives. The calling of womanhood is a divine commission to bring forth and cultivate life, to glorify the majesty of the Father and the Son, to enlarge one's God-given destiny through obedience and valor, and to help plant in the souls of the children of God the seeds of power unfolding through the blessings of the gospel. Across generations of time, women of obedience have taught through deeds of service how we can choose to help the infinite grow within us in fulfillment of God's design of mercy and enlightenment.

1. ONE MOMENT IN ETERNITY: MARY, MOTHER OF JESUS

Over two millennia ago, Mary, the mother of Jesus, fulfilled a mission of great dignity. Only one woman in all eternity received and fulfilled the calling to bring forth the Son of God into mortality. What a sublime commission of womanhood that was! In choosing to fulfill her majestic calling, Mary responded in full harmony with the role assigned to her from the Father and performed it with exemplary honor. It was a role that embraced both joy and anguish, supreme happiness and monumental suffering—but the everlasting memory of her devoted service is the crowning glory of her priceless contribution toward the enactment of the redeeming Atonement of her son, Jesus Christ. Thus Mary can rise among all women as an exemplar of majesty.

The account of her choice to fulfill her divine calling to magnify the Lord is recorded in the familiar verses of the first chapter of Luke. Can we look back and imagine her feelings, desires, and memories as she grasped the importance of her calling and embraced the will of her Father in Heaven? Perhaps we can consider the following scene of possibilities and let it shed light on our own desire to do better in the world:

> She looked about in the dimness of the evening. The glow of a candle brought alive the objects in her humble room: a shawl lying across the cot, a small segment of bread on the table. Moments ago, this small world had been illuminated by the dazzling radiance of a heavenly messenger delivering an annunciation, magnificent and unfathomable.
>
> Her heart was still beating with vigor after his departure. Her thoughts soared into the eternities. She rubbed her hands softly together in search of comfort. What had he said? "Hail, thou that art highly favoured, the Lord is with thee: blessed art thou among women."[1] She was still pondering this stirring message, asking perhaps, "How could I be blessed among women? I am but a simple girl of the lineage of David."[2]

But in answer to her inner questions, her heavenly visitor had opened to her a vista of astounding glory: "Fear not, Mary: for thou hast found favour with God. And, behold, thou shalt conceive in thy womb, and bring forth a son, and shalt call his name Jesus. He shall be great, and shall be called the Son of the Highest: and the Lord God shall give unto him the throne of his father David: And he shall reign over the house of Jacob for ever; and of his kingdom there shall be no end."[3]

Recalling these poignant words, her mind danced with joyful anticipation. To be the mother of the Son of God? To raise up the great King as promised over the generations? To be blessed among women? How shall this be? The words of the angel again flowed into her memory with compelling truth: "For with God nothing shall be impossible."[4] To this she had responded with words of humble acceptance: "Behold the handmaid of the Lord; be it unto me according to thy word."[5] And then the angel had departed from her presence.

She stood alone, perhaps smiling in remembrance of the words of Isaiah: "For unto us a child is born, unto us a son is given: and the government shall be upon his shoulder: and his name shall be called Wonderful, Counsellor, The mighty God, The everlasting Father, The Prince of Peace."[6] She knew her people had been looking forward for generations to the day when such a promise would be realized. But the time was not in the distant future. The time was *now*.

She must surely have felt waves of comfort and peace flowing through her being. She knew that something new, something wonderful, something magnificent was about to happen as a blessing from heaven unto the world. The Messiah would soon be born and come into her arms. It would be her sublime blessing to raise Him and lift Him toward His divine station. She looked upward in the dimness of her room with a profound sense of gratitude, as if peering into heaven.

Not long thereafter she would share her feelings with her cousin Elisabeth: "My soul doth magnify the Lord, And my spirit hath rejoiced in God my Saviour."[7] No doubt she would remember forever these words about magnifying the Lord, and she would likely share them with others throughout her life in the spirit of love and eternal motherhood. Her witness would be anchored in the healing testimony planted in her soul:

For he hath regarded the low estate of his handmaiden: for, behold, from henceforth all generations shall call me blessed.

For he that is mighty hath done to me great things; and holy is his name.

And his mercy is on them that fear him from generation to generation.[8]

In her sweetness and love, Mary became the mother of Jesus Christ, a divine commission of majesty and honor. With devotion, she and her husband, Joseph, nurtured and raised their son in preparation for His heavenly mission of redemption. Mary's witness would continually confirm her decision to honor God in humble obedience and encourage others to do the same: "Whatsoever he saith unto you, do it" (John 2:5). She would stand at the foot of the cross when Jesus would give His loving directive for her nurture and care: "When Jesus therefore saw his mother, and the disciple standing by, whom he loved, he saith unto his mother, Woman, behold thy son! Then saith he to the disciple [John], Behold thy mother! And from that hour that disciple took her unto his own home" (John 19:26–27).

Finally, Mary would also be present with the disciples in the upper room following the Ascension: "These all continued with one accord in prayer and supplication, with the women, and Mary the mother of Jesus, and with his brethren" (Acts 1:14). From the beginning until the end, she would honor her eternal mission with valor and womanly glory as an unforgettable example of virtue and divine majesty.

Though our own lives are at times touched with tribulation, though we face repeated challenges in fulfilling our callings and duties, we can remember the words shared with Mary: "For with God nothing shall be impossible" (Luke 1:37). As sons and daughters of God, we can take to heart the example of Mary, mother of Jesus, and go forward in the strength of the Lord.

2. *Sisterly Echoes: Mothers of the Stripling Warriors*

The majesty of Mary is an all-embracing dimension of eternal womanhood also reflected in the lives of many other women through the ages. Among those are the mothers of the stripling warriors in the Book of Mormon. Theirs is an account of the triumph of liberty over the incursion of enemies bent on destroying religious freedom and extinguishing the glory of the gospel of Jesus Christ. The courage of the stripling warriors is celebrated in the scriptural account contained in the book of Alma, especially chapters 53 through 57. As we will see, two familiar passages confirm that they were acting in accordance with the counsel and instruction of their mothers (see Alma 56:47–48; 57:21).

The abridged account does not contain details about the hours and days and years the mothers spent teaching their sons principles of faith and courage. We treasure the in-depth record of the instructions given by Lehi and Alma to their children, but we have only a glimpse of the words from the mothers of the stripling warriors. Perhaps someday in the future, these stories and many other truths will be shared with us as a blessing from heaven, for Mormon said: "Behold, I was about to write them, all which were engraven upon the plates of Nephi, but the Lord forbade it, saying: I will try the faith of my people" (3 Nephi 26:11).

In the meantime, can we imagine a conversation between one of the mothers and her young son as he prepared to enter the arena of battle to protect his family and the nation? Perhaps the following scene will provide a framework of encouragement for all of us—mothers and fathers, grandmothers and grandfathers—as we seek to uphold the principles of the gospel and share them with our loved ones who face daunting challenges:

> The light of dawn streamed through the windows of their humble dwelling in Jershon. They stood together in silence, face to face—mother and son—awaiting the beckoning sound of a distant trumpet that would soon call a small army of young men into service for the liberty of their people. She stroked his locks. He smiled and drew her toward him into a fond embrace.
>
> "Your father would be so proud of you," she whispered. "He gave his life in honoring his oath and covenant of peace."[9]
>
> "My friends and I have a new covenant," replied her son in gentle tones. "A covenant to assemble ourselves and rise up to fight for the liberty of the Nephites and to protect the land unto the laying down of our lives, just as my father did."[10]
>
> She closed her eyes and took his hands in hers. "I hear in my heart the whisperings of the Spirit that the Lord will protect you as you follow His guidance and the leadership of Helaman."
>
> "Helaman is also like a father to me,"[11] replied her son. "He has softened the anguish of our people in our compassion for their Nephite hosts[12] and dissuaded our fathers from suspending their oath to abandon their weapons of war.[13] He is a man of honor. He

has protected us. And I will do my part." The young man stood firm and placed his hand upon the crest of his sword.

His mother nodded and breathed a deep sigh of gratitude. "Helaman is our guardian," she replied. "He is a noble father unto you and your friends. And yet the father who is highest of all is your Father in Heaven. You know what your weapon of victory will be. It will be your truth and soberness, your obedience to the commandments of God, and your willingness to walk uprightly before Him."[14]

"I believe you, Mother," responded her son. "I will always remember your lesson that if I never doubt, God will deliver me and my fellow soldiers."[15]

"Will you promise me that you will return to my side in honor and safety?" she asked.

"I will return," he declared with resolve. "And you and our people will be free."

At that moment, a trumpet sounded in the distance. The noise of marching steps echoed in rhythm with the notes. Voices filled the air. Scurrying sounds resonated in the background.

"They are coming near!" the son exclaimed. "It is time for me to join with the army!" He picked up his supplies and prepared to leave. "I love you, Mother." He kissed her tenderly on the forehead.

"Be safe, my son," she replied quietly. "Stand fast in that liberty wherewith God has made [you] free."[16]

"Because of your example, I will remember the Lord my God every day, and keep his statutes, and his commandments continually.[17] Great blessings will flow unto our people."

She watched him walk through the door to join with his compatriots in the service of the people of the Lord. In joyous strains, she called out after him, "Strong is your faith, and without limit is your courage!"

Over the next weeks and months the stripling warriors of the people of Ammon would perform courageous service in the face of peril at the hands of their enemies. Helaman's mantra to them on the cusp of battle had been in the form of a question: "Therefore what say ye, my sons, will ye go against them to battle?"[18] The answer is summarized with dramatic power in Helaman's letter to Captain Moroni, the commanding general of the Lord's people:

And now I say unto you, my beloved brother Moroni, that never had I seen so great courage, nay, not amongst all the Nephites. . . .

Now they never had fought, yet they did not fear death; and they did think more upon the liberty of their fathers than they did upon their lives; yea, they had been taught by their mothers, that if they did not doubt, God would deliver them.

And they rehearsed unto me the words of their mothers, saying: We do not doubt our mothers knew it.[19]

What the young sons had learned from their nurturing mothers would unfold in majestic courage, for they were "exceedingly valiant for courage, and . . . were true at all times in whatsoever thing they were entrusted."[20] Concerning their victorious achievements, Helaman would later exclaim, "Yea, never were men known to have fought with such miraculous strength; and with such mighty power."[21] He extolled their ability to remain "firm and undaunted. Yea, and they did obey and observe to perform every word of command with exactness; yea, and even according to their faith it was done unto them; and I did remember the words which they said unto me that their mothers had taught them."[22]

Miraculously, despite serious injuries in combat, none of the two thousand young warriors nor the additional sixty of their peers added during the fray of battle[23] lost their lives. How did this success come about? In a lesson for all humanity, Helaman confirmed the truth:

And we do justly ascribe it to the miraculous power of God, because of their exceeding faith in that which they had been taught [by their mothers] to believe—that there was a just God, and whosoever did not doubt, that they should be preserved by his marvelous power.

Now this was the faith of these of whom I have spoken; they are young, and their minds are firm, and they do put their trust in God continually.[24]

The decision of their mothers to teach principles of endurance and faith bore the fruit of stalwart courage. The record reports that the young warriors and their leader did continually "pour out our souls in prayer to God, that he would strengthen us and deliver us out of the hands of our enemies, yea, and also give us strength that we might retain our cities, and our lands, and our possessions, for the support of our people."[25] In response to their prayers, the Lord our God did visit us with assurances that he would deliver us; yea, insomuch that he did speak peace to our souls, and did grant unto us great faith, and did cause us that we should hope for our deliverance in him. And we did take courage with our small force which we had received, and were fixed with a determination to conquer our enemies, and to maintain our lands, and our possessions, and our wives, and our children, and the cause of our liberty.[26]

The role played by the mothers of the stripling warriors is an example for all of us today. In the words of President Ezra Taft Benson: "These marvelous mothers taught them to put on the whole armor of God, to place their trust in the Lord, and to doubt not. By so doing, not one of these young men was lost" (*Come, Listen to a Prophet's Voice* [Deseret Book: Salt Lake City, 1990], 1–2). The decision of the mothers to teach their sons the principle of deliverance anticipates the very role exemplified by Mary, mother of Jesus. Not many years later, Mary would be called upon to ensure that the life of her son Immanuel would unfold as a divine means to deliver and save the entire human race through the power of the Atonement.

> "All the sons and daughters of God can rise above tribulation when they decide in faith to press forward in the service of the Lord."

Eternal womanhood in such inspiring manifestations is an unforgettable confirmation of how this principle can also be applied today in our lives. Yes, there will be challenges to face and overcome, but all the sons and daughters of God can rise above tribulation when they decide in faith to press forward in the service of the Lord. Eternal womanhood and divine majesty are of the same spirit, the same essence, and the same power—all partaking in the work and glory of the Father and the Son for the blessing and eternal life of mankind.

3. A MODERN MOMENT: SAVING THE WORD OF GOD

The resolve of women such as Mary and the mothers of the stripling warriors to honor and magnify their duties—despite the influences acting against them—is a confirmation of the blessings of the Lord to bring about miracles in the lives of His sons and daughters. How do we feel about the opportunities all around us to choose majesty over mediocrity and devotion over complacency? What follows is a scene based on an actual event from the days of the Restoration that can resonate well in confirming the workings of the divine in our daily lives. Perhaps this episode, involving a modern Mary, will raise questions in our minds and hearts about the decisions we can make—despite the challenges we face— to do a little better each day in building the kingdom of God on the earth:

Strange metallic noises echoed through the air amidst gruff laughter and muffled shouts. Clouds of dust were billowing through a broken window of the building's upper story. Thumping and smashing from invisible sources persevered painfully across the dismal scene.

Two young girls, eyes staring, hearts pounding, crouched together in the shadows near a corner of the fence a short distance away. Mary held her younger sister Caroline close to her and pointed toward a dark figure appearing through a side door. He was balancing an armload of papers in his arms. As he emerged into the light, he launched his load into the air, where it completed its trajectory and smashed into the dirt with a loud thud, sending up plumes of dust all around. In a fit of sinister laughter, he motioned to his comrades appearing behind him at the door and then pointed to the scattered papers on the ground. "Here are the Mormon Commandments!"[27]

Mary whispered to her sister, "You recognize these men, don't you?"

Caroline nodded and replied with trembling words, "Yes. The same ones who smashed the windows in our home the other night and tore down the roof. We need to run away right now!"[28]

Gently, Mary placed her finger against her sister's lips to signal silence. "Let's wait just a minute."

Within the older sister's mind there must have churned a flood of conflicting feelings: on the one hand anguish to witness the recorded revelations from a living prophet being mercilessly destroyed; on the other hand, relief in recalling a mental image of the same prophet, who just over three years ago in Kirtland had laid his hands softly upon her head—a humble twelve-year-old girl—and pronounced a great blessing, the first she had ever received. He then had graciously permitted her to retain a

borrowed copy of the Book of Mormon that had filled her with
spiritual nourishment of heavenly blessings.[29]

Previous to that, she had savored the rousing words of priesthood leaders concerning the magnificence of the Restoration as
they declared "a powerful testimony, by the Holy Spirit, of the
truth of the great work they were engaged in; and which they were
commissioned by the Father to present to all the world."[30]

As the current scene of vile destruction played out before her
eyes, her inner soul most likely recalled the soothing emotions she
had felt while consuming the wisdom of the Book of Mormon as
a newly converted member of the Church: "If any person in this
world was ever perfectly happy in the possession of any coveted
treasure, I was when I had permission to read that wonderful
book."[31]

In the fall of 1831, when she was but thirteen years of age, her
family had moved here to Independence, Jackson County, Missouri,
to make a new home in Zion. Perhaps Mary was shivering now
with the sensations of her memories since then—joy and terror,
hope and fear. How would it now end?

Caroline squeezed Mary's hand with fear, but Mary stroked
her hair and smiled. "We have a work to do," she whispered.

We can imagine that the words of Church leaders were seeping
again through her mind with refreshing comfort. What they had
told her not too long ago continued to foster courage in her heart,
for they confirmed that the Prophet's revelations "had not been
printed as yet, but few had looked upon them, for they were in
large sheets, not folded. They spoke of [the revelations] with such
reverence, as coming from the Lord; they felt to rejoice that they
were counted worthy to be the means of publishing them for the
benefit of the whole world. While talking they were filled with
the spirit."[32] Then, on that same occasion, young Mary had also
borne her testimony of the truth of what they were saying, for
she had prayed to the Lord for understanding about the divine
happenings unfolding around her and declared, "I felt the spirit
of it in a moment."

"Caroline," whispered Mary, "we need to gather those papers
and save them from the mob. Those papers contain the divine word
of God and are a blessing for our families and the whole world."

Two years younger than her sister, Caroline gulped at the thought, saying words to this effect: "Mary, if you go to get any of them, I will go, too. But they will kill us."[33]

Mary lifted up her head and smiled. "We can do it safely—in the strength of the Lord."

Hands clasped together, the two of them watched closely until the mobsters became distracted tearing down a wall of the building. At that moment, the girls raced from their hiding place, scooped up armfuls of the printed papers, and propelled themselves toward an opening in the fence behind the building.

Two of the hoodlums shouted for them to stop as they disappeared through the fence and raced into a neighboring corn field, pursued closely by the enemy. With the corn five to six feet high, the girls continued their flight under protection of Mother Nature's abundance. Soon they found a secluded spot among the corn plants some distance away. In contrast to the sickening fumes smoldering around the scene from which they had fled, the nurturing scent of the ripening harvest offered pleasant relief.

At that moment, Mary might have whispered to her sister, "I think we should lay the papers on the ground and then hide them by lying down on them." That is precisely what they did.

They waited in silence until the ominous rustling noise of their chasers began to fade and grow quieter until it evaporated altogether. Then nothing was left—except the peaceful silence around the daughters of the Lord and His printed word. The girls rose slowly, gathered their treasure in their arms, and made their way across the landscape in a direction leading away from the destruction.

"We have saved the Lord's word," said Mary. "We have a bit of heaven to share now with others."

Soon they came upon an old log stable, where they found the wife and children of the printer, W. W. Phelps, looking for refuge after their house had been pillaged. Sister Phelps received the papers—The Book of Commandments[34]—with joy. Mary later was given a copy of the bound revelations and prized it for the rest of her life as a majestic treasure from heaven.[35]

Some four years after the recovery of the Book of Commandments on that memorable day, Mary Elizabeth Rollins married Adam Lightner and began her own family life. She transcended stressful future years of adversity with courage. On one occasion near Far West, she refused to abandon her friends who had been ordered to be killed, saying: "I refuse to go, for where they die, I will die, for I am a full-blooded Mormon, and I am not ashamed to own it."[36] When the authorities instead arrested Joseph Smith and his brother Hyrum, the people were spared, though bathed in anguish.

During the ensuing years, Mary helped sustain her growing family circle through seamstress work and giving art classes. She survived momentous hardships with valor and eventually journeyed with her family to Utah, where she spent her remaining years as a loyal mother in Zion and a faithful witness of the divine blessings that flow from a loving and merciful Father in Heaven. Her service radiates as an example of those who, in divine majesty, choose to "bear witness to the words of the glorious Majesty on high, to whom be glory forever and ever. Amen."[37]

PONDERING

The courageous choices of Mary of Nazareth, the mothers of the stripling warriors, and young Mary Elizabeth Rollins are reminders that all of us have opportunities to follow the Spirit in righteousness and receive blessings of divine majesty. As you ponder and pray to develop this quality, consider the following questions:

- In what ways has the Lord helped you to magnify your callings in life with honor?

- What feelings have come to you while helping others to understand the majesty of God and the power of His divine gospel plan?

- In what ways can you best fulfill your desire to discover and share with others the presence of the divine in daily life?

- How can you bear your testimony of the restored gospel with greater authenticity and power?

- How does the spirit of gratitude for life and hope enrich your family relationships?

- In what ways has the strength of the Lord enabled you to overcome trials and challenges and guide others to do the same through your example and encouragement?

- How do the words of the angel unto Mary—"For with God nothing shall be impossible"—bring greater hope and strength into your life?

- How do the words of the mothers of the stripling warriors—"that if they did not doubt, God would deliver them"—resonate in your life and in the lives of your family members?

- Concerning the Book of Mormon, Mary Elizabeth Rollins said, "If any person in this world was ever perfectly happy in the possession of any coveted treasure I was when I had permission to read that wonderful book." How do these words inspire you to do a little better each day in reading the Book of Mormon and sharing with others your witness of its truth?

- Have you felt peace and tranquility as you have lived the gospel? How might those feelings be compared to an awakening of your soul? How can you draw strength from those feelings to help you magnify your callings?

- How does the example of eternal womanhood in this chapter help you to confirm and experience the majesty of the divine in your life?

- In what ways can you help others have this same blessing in greater measure?

CHAPTER TWO

Loyal Love

For whither thou goest, I will go; and where thou lodgest, I
will lodge: thy people shall be my people, and thy God my God.
(Ruth 1:16)

JESUS CONFIRMED THE IMPORTANCE OF love in our lives: "Thou shalt love the Lord thy God with all thy heart, and with all thy soul, and with all thy mind. This is the first and great commandment. And the second is like unto it, Thou shalt love thy neighbour as thyself" (Matthew 22:37–39). God loves us with a perfect love, "for God is love" (1 John 4:8). This principle teaches us to love Him with all our heart, might, mind, and strength, just as we are to love others. Loyal love is the motivating power of our divine mission to teach the gospel. Loyal love is the substance of everlasting life. Loyal love is the key to eternal hope and peace, and it is the binding connection between God and His children. The gospel of Jesus Christ is founded upon the principle of enduring love. Love of this kind marks the pathway to salvation through the Atonement of Jesus Christ: "For God so loved the world, that he gave his only begotten Son, that whosoever believeth in him should not perish, but have everlasting life" (John 3:16).

> " Loyalty and love are eternal partners. "

As we look around us on a daily basis, we can see that loyalty and love are eternal partners. We find evidence in the lives of those we honor and respect that abiding love preserves enduring loyalty. We feel the comfort of the Spirit when we show our love for others through renewed support for their wellbeing and happiness.

Loyal love is the mark of divine perfection. Even though the sons and daughters of God are not perfect, they can aspire to overcome their weaknesses and follow in the footsteps of the Savior toward a more perfect state of wholeness. Shortly before His atoning sacrifice, the Savior said to His disciples, "But that the world may know that I love the Father; and as the Father gave me commandment, even so I do. Arise, let us go hence" (John 14:31). "Arise, let us go hence" is a humbling and inspiring invitation to follow the words of the Lord in our own personal lives, for He said to us all, "Come, follow me" (Luke 18:22).

In His final intercessory prayer, He besought the Father to bless and unify His followers, "that the world may know that thou hast sent me, and hast loved them, as thou hast loved me" (John 17:23). The Lord's counsel to be loyal to the Father and to make love the central focus of our lives is central to cultivating a more spiritual way of life.

In so many ways, the role of eternal womanhood is to lift up before the world a radiant ensign of loyal love. A week after he organized the Relief Society on March 17, 1842, the Prophet Joseph Smith visited again with the women of the Church and subsequently recorded thoughts in his journal about their example of service, noting that their circle included

> some of our most intelligent, humane, philanthropic, and respectable ladies; and we are well assured from a knowledge of those pure principles of benevolence that flow spontaneously from their humane and philanthropic bosoms, that with the resources they will have at command, they will fly to the relief of the stranger; they will pour in oil and wine to the wounded heart of the distressed; they will dry up the tears of the orphan and make the widow's heart to rejoice. . . . [T]hey have always been ready to open their doors to the weary traveler, to divide their scant pittance with the hungry, and from their robbed and impoverished wardrobes, to divide with the more needy and destitute. (*HC* 4:567–568)

Down through the ages, many of the daughters of the Lord have displayed abiding and loyal love to their families and all of the children of God within their circle of influence. A grand example of that is Ruth, whose statement to her mother-in-law, beginning with the words "for whither thou goest, I will go" (Ruth 1:16), is an unforgettable witness of loyalty and love. The beautiful hymn "I'll Go Where You Want Me to Go" (*Hymns*, no. 270) celebrates her life of service. We have in the four chapters of the book of Ruth a few details of her life and times. But how can we journey back through the ages and imagine being an observer of her trials and triumphs, challenges and victories? Perhaps the following scenes will open up a doorway to that possibility. Perhaps these scenes will awaken within you some familiar memories of your own experiences in giving service to others and showing them an expression of your own loyal love.

1. ONE MOMENT IN ETERNITY: RUTH
A. Sunset

Three widows. Three broken hearts. Three figures stood together, side-by-side—the noble matriarch and two choice younger women—looking across the expanse of golden grain fields of Moab toward the setting sun, their shadows lengthening silently behind them toward the east.

"Ten years,"[38] whispered the older woman, a spirit of melancholy sentiment reverberating in her voice. "My husband brought us here to escape the famine in Judah—and then another famine crept into our family with his sudden death."[39]

The three remained silent as the winds of the plains caressed their cheeks. "Then," she continued, "my two sons followed in his footsteps. Ten years in Moab. I thank the Lord that you two choice daughters of the land can join with me in healing our broken hearts."

The silhouette of a bird circling in the distance crossed over the fading archway of the disappearing sun. "Mother," said one of the young women quietly, "you are the strength to our souls and the comfort to our hearts. How can we find joy again unless we have the blessing of your presence?"

Naomi responded with tenderness, "Go, return each to [your] mother's house: the Lord deal kindly with you, as ye have dealt with the dead, and with me."[40]

A look of anxiety clung to the faces of the two younger women. Smiling with compassion, their mother-in-law uttered the promising words, "The Lord grant you that ye may find rest, each of you in the house of her husband."[41] She then kissed them both; and they lifted up their voices and wept.[42]

When the two daughters regained their composure, they ventured a response, almost in the format of a melodious duet, "Surely we will return with thee unto thy people."[43]

The matriarch radiated gratitude as their yearning for unity unfolded before her eyes. She brushed away her tears and shared with them ideas from her inner concerns: that her senior years had caused to evaporate into the sunset of life any hope for providing new husbands for the widowed daughters and that the hand of the Lord would more gently bless them with a new life in their own homeland.

One of the young women threw her arms around Naomi and held her tightly for an extended time. Then, giving her a farewell kiss, she took up her satchel of belongings and headed toward the nearby village where her family home was awaiting her. Her two companions watched as she slowly faded away into the shadows of the evening, stopping only for a moment to wave a final good-bye before vanishing forever.

"And now, my daughter," the matriarch said to the remaining young woman, "what shall become of you?"

At that moment, Ruth turned and lovingly embraced her mother-in-law[44] as she found the courage to voice the decision that had been unfolding in her heart for a good long while. In words that have since become the mantra of loyalty and love, she spoke with radiant inspiration and unstoppable resolve:

> Entreat me not to leave thee, or to return from following after thee: for whither thou goest, I will go; and where thou lodgest, I will lodge: thy people shall be my people, and thy God my God:
>
> Where thou diest, will I die, and there will I be buried: the Lord do so to me, and more also, if ought but death part thee and me.[45]

In that soothing moment, the two of them felt the vision of a new world simmering within their hearts with a beckoning glow. Cleaving to one another, they gazed toward the purple haze of the western sky and looked forward to a dawning of joy over Bethlehem.

B. Dawning of a New Day

Ruth reached down and lifted up a stalk of wheat left lying on the ground by the reapers. In her hands, she gently rubbed the head of the stalk, bringing out into the autumn air the individual grains of wheat. Fingering them into a small circle on the palm of her hand, she smiled, surely feeling peace in her heart and contentment in her mind. We can imagine her whispering quiet words: "These kernels are emblems of my family—my family now and my family to come as a blessing of the Lord."

The sunlight of morning coaxed a film of perspiration to settle upon her forehead as she continued gleaning in the harvest field lying on the outskirts of Bethlehem. Her thoughts flowed again and again through her mind. "How kind and gracious are these people. How welcoming have they been to a Moabite widow from a different country and a different culture."

Across the field she could see a distinguished man guiding the reapers in their service. It was Boaz, the same man who had offered her water to quench her thirst[46] and bread to still her hunger.[47] His words of friendship still echoed in her ears: "The Lord recompense thy work, and a full reward be given thee of the Lord God of Israel, under whose wings thou art come to trust."[48]

She knew he had encouraged the reapers to leave an abundance of grain for her to gather, even from the best sheaves of the field.[49] How pleased she was to observe her satchel of grain expand. No doubt she envisioned herself returning home once again that evening to render nurture unto her beloved mother-in-law, the very one who had encouraged her to remain close to the man in charge of the field.

The recent words of Naomi concerning this man, a relative of her deceased husband, kept circling through the mind of the young widow: "Blessed be he of the Lord, who hath not left off his kindness to the living and to the dead."[50] Perhaps she savored now more than just an inkling that her service as a stranger[51] would soon include service as a wife and mother in a circle of harmony, loyalty, and love.

C. Vision of the Future

Sometime later, this gentle Ruth, with peace and eternal contentment in her heart, looked over toward her newly born child asleep in the arms of Naomi. The young mother smiled in humble gratitude. A stream of memories flowed across her mind: how she had mourned in her native land over the loss of her young husband, son of Naomi, and how her mother-in-law had given her blessings of comfort and love in those dire times, showering her with kindness so dear and so abundant as to awaken the spirit of enduring joy in her life.[52]

The new mother looked into the faces of the neighborly women assembled in the room as they gazed at the child and whispered words of fondness and delight. Ruth was amazed at the welcoming arms of hospitality extended to her by these choice sisters upon her arrival from Moab over a year earlier. Now, once more, she could partake of their voices of friendship and their spirit of warmth within the family circle.

A bouquet of flowers resting beside her on the table reminded her of the fragrance of the nature in which she was immersed while laboring in the fields of Boaz. With gladness she had received his affection and now whispered to herself once again his words of comfort leading to their marriage: "And now, my daughter, fear not; I will do to thee all that thou requirest: for all the city of my people doth know that thou art a virtuous woman."[53]

The vision of her son asleep before her eyes blessed her with a sublime reminder of God's eternal blessings to His children of Israel—including His children adopted from other cultures. The women of the community had spoken well concerning the lineage of heaven unfolding before their eyes—that this child named Obed[54] (meaning "serving," "worshipping") would extend the reach of Israel over the generations—even to the future Messiah of the world.[55]

A tear of gladness rolled down her cheek. She spoke a silent prayer of thanksgiving as she closed her eyes to peer into the future. She perceived in her mind's eye a light of glory rising above the horizon of time—the dawning of an era of promised redemption.

Ruth (meaning "friend" or "companion") is an exceptional prototype of a woman who epitomizes the qualities of loyal and enduring love. Truly she serves as a model of ideal womanhood (see Thomas S. Monson, "Models to Follow," *Ensign*, Nov. 2002, 60). She radiates a spirit of holiness, hope, honor, and harmony—being a key participant in the lineage of David (her future great-grandson) and the mortal Messiah. Ruth is specifically named in Matthew's unfolding of the generations of Christ (see Matthew 1:5).

Her story is an emblem of conversion, of humbly deciding to set aside one's former ways in favor of a new and higher pattern of living aligned with the spiritual laws of Jehovah. She is the model of transition from a culture on the fringes of Israelite society to one that embraced her fully with charity and hospitality as a daughter of God.

2. *SISTERLY ECHOES: SAMARITAN WOMAN BY THE WELL*

More than a millennium after the time of Ruth, there occurred another memorable event where another non-Israelite woman displayed loyal love for higher truth. A few details of the visit of the Samaritan woman with Jesus Christ during His mortal ministry are given in the fourth chapter of the Gospel of John. Her life-changing experience might well have unfolded as in the following scene:

> "Why this way?" she whispered to herself as she picked her way along the stone-infested pathway leading far beyond the outskirts of the town.[56] Clinging tightly to the water pot balanced under her arm, she slowed her pace while pondering an uneasy conflict in her mind. She knew that it was easier to fetch water from one of the wells back near her home. But she felt impressed this day to go out to Jacob's well, a good distance away.[57]
>
> "Is it just because the water out there seems fresher and cleaner?" she asked herself. "Or is there some other reason?"
>
> Seeking a reconciliation, she raised her eyes toward the western horizon and allowed the familiar view to flow again into her soul: a noble mountain rising into the sky as an ensign of truth.[58] A feeling of comfort unleashed itself as she surveyed the summit above the steep face of the mount and allowed the history of her culture to stream once again through her mind: atop that peak they had been worshipping the Almighty for generations and dreaming of a day when the Messiah would return in glory to bless their lives.
>
> Peace flooded her soul as she quickened her pace toward the well coming into view far off in the distance. The noonday sun caused beads of perspiration to form on her brow—perspiration that expanded when she spotted silhouettes of figures also down the rocky road. Who were these robed individuals coming toward her? Her heart skipped a beat as she recognized them—Jewish priestly officials, emblems of the enmity that had existed for centuries between her Samaritan culture and that of the Jewish way of life.[59]

She recoiled far to the right of the roadway as the group approached her, buzzing among themselves with muted conversation. Should she be concerned for her own safety? "Are they conspiring against me as a lonely Samaritan woman?" With eyes lowered in pretense that the forthcoming enemy did not exist, she allowed them to pass by her and continue on their way toward the town.

Sighing with relief, she hurried onward toward Jacob's well, feeling a rush of consolation to be approaching a holy site where history still maintained a spirit of aliveness in the minds of those who stopped there for the quenching of thirst. She felt confirmed in her decision to come here this day. She also felt a sense of compassion to be able to draw water from this sacred well to share with her family. She mused that perhaps it was that sense of loyalty to family that was at the heart of her motivation this day.

But then, as she approached the well, she again felt a shock to spot another robed individual sitting alone alongside the well, watching her with focused eyes. Who was this? What might his purpose be?

Immediately she learned the answer, for the stranger, in his nobility and peacefulness, spoke calmly unto her, "Give me to drink."[60]

Somewhat relieved, she responded, "How is it that thou, being a Jew, askest drink of me, which am a woman of Samaria? for the Jews have no dealings with the Samaritans."

The answer she then absorbed raised a chill of expectation within her heart. "If thou knewest the gift of God," He said to her, "and who it is that saith to thee, Give me to drink; thou wouldest have asked of him, and he would have given thee living water."

With a tingling sense of courage, she then pointed toward her water pot and responded, "Sir, thou hast nothing to draw with, and the well is deep: from whence then hast thou that living water? Art thou greater than our father Jacob, which gave us the well, and drank thereof himself, and his children, and his cattle?"

His response lifted her spirits in a transcendent way: "Whosoever drinketh of this water shall thirst again," He declared, "But whosoever drinketh of the water that I shall give him shall never thirst; but the water that I shall give him shall be in him a well of water springing up into everlasting life."

Raising her head in anticipation, she then spoke in a receptive tone: "Sir, give me this water, that I thirst not, neither come hither to draw."

Smiling at her, He softly responded, "Go, call thy husband, and come hither."

"I have no husband," she admitted, whereupon the kindly Stranger confirmed her status and shared with her secrets about her personal situation that He could not have known about, unless . . .

"Sir," she uttered in a tone of astonishment, "I perceive that thou art a prophet. Our fathers worshipped in this mountain; and ye say, that in Jerusalem is the place where men ought to worship."

Then into her waiting ears flowed words of divine prophecy: "Woman, believe me, the hour cometh, when ye shall neither in this mountain, nor yet at Jerusalem, worship the Father. Ye worship ye know not what: we know what we worship: for salvation is of the Jews. But the hour cometh, and now is, when the true worshippers shall worship the Father in spirit and in truth: for the Father seeketh such to worship him."

At that moment, she began to have a growing sense of why, on this day, she had come so far to seek water.

The radiant individual facing her, no longer seeming to be a stranger, added these words of wisdom about authentic worship: "For unto such hath God promised his Spirit. And they who worship him, must worship in spirit and in truth."[61]

With a renewed sense of hope, she responded, "I know that Messias cometh, which is called Christ: when he is come, he will tell us all things."

He then said unto her words that confirmed her anticipation: "I that speak unto thee am he."

In that instant, the dialogue was interrupted by the sounds of an approaching throng. The woman turned to recognize the very group of gentlemen who had passed her by as she was walking toward Jacob's well. The men, holding parcels of provisions they had acquired in town, were astonished to find the same woman speaking with their Master.

But she was not astonished to find them rejoining Him, for she now knew who He was, and she was filled with a loyal commitment to rush back into the town and announce the arrival of the Messiah her people had been waiting for. Leaving her water pot behind, she quickly returned to share the good news of the gospel of living water with her friends. The story of Jesus and the woman at the well is a confirmation of the universal love of the Lord for all peoples.[62]

Said the Savior to His disciples after the woman's departure, "Lift up your eyes, and look on the fields; for they are white already to harvest" (John 4:35). Because of the testimony of the woman before her fellow citizens, they flocked out to meet the Savior—and the harvest continued. Many of the Samaritans in that city came to believe in the Savior according to the witness of the woman. They supplicated the Lord to remain with them for a time, and He spent two days with them, causing many more to receive a personal witness of the truth of His words.

" She became an enduring emblem of the eternal womanhood that reaches out to bless the sons and daughters of God in all cultures and all ends of the earth. "

Unto the woman, the latest converts said in gratitude, "Now we believe, not because of thy saying: for we have heard him ourselves, and know that this is indeed the Christ, the Saviour of the world" (John 4:42).

Through her loving acceptance, the woman at the well, despite her earlier waywardness in life (see John 4:17–18), was awakened and quickened by the Spirit of the Lord. She became an enduring emblem of the eternal womanhood that reaches out to bless the sons and daughters of God in all cultures and all ends of the earth. All of the sons and daughters of God have the opportunity to follow her example by responding in faith and loyalty to the Lord's invitation: "Come, follow me" (Luke 18:22).

3. A MODERN MOMENT: CALLED ON A MISSION OF LOVE
The highest blessings of the Lord flow unto His faithful and loyal children. If circumstances beyond their control hinder or delay their obedience, He consoles them by accepting their sincere offerings until the day comes that their mission can be completed (see D&C 124:49–54). The following true account by a member of a stake presidency confirms this truth:

The appointed hour had arrived, and all those invited to attend were now present. We were gathered together in a small room at the back of the chapel building overlooking the lush landscape of the fields stretching out to the north. All of us in the group were smiling. Feelings of joy prevailed. It was my privilege and honor this day to set apart several stake missionaries who had been called to serve.

After setting apart one middle-aged sister (we'll call her Sister Brown), I noticed that she was in tears. Following the session, I asked her if all was well. She told me the story behind her emotion.

Many years ago, she had been called to serve a full-time mission, but circumstances had prevented her from going. She had always felt she had relinquished important blessings, since a mission was mentioned in her patriarchal blessing.

Her tears on this day were tears of joy, since the setting-apart blessing included statements that were, as she put it, "word-for-word" from her patriarchal blessing. Thus Sister Brown knew that her Father in Heaven loved her and had reserved for her the blessings He wanted her to have through faithful service. In the same measure, her abiding and loyal love for the Lord and His children was now blossoming in the form of active service. By accepting this new calling, Sister Brown learned that the gateway had been opened for the fulfillment of her patriarchal blessing.

She saw and heard and felt a warming confirmation that the Lord always watches over us and wants us to know of His abiding love and concern. As Paul quotes from Isaiah, "But as it is written, Eye hath not seen, nor ear heard, neither have entered into the heart of man, the things which God hath prepared for them that love him. But God hath revealed *them* unto us by his Spirit: for the Spirit searcheth all things, yea, the deep things of God."[63]

From stories such as this one—and many others we experience personally—we learn of the mercy and compassion of the Lord. And we can learn that the opportunity is open for us all to serve the Lord faithfully through loyal love and devotion. This is a tender message we can also share with others. Why? Because we love them and have a burning desire to bear our testimony that the Lord loves them with a perfect love and wants them to be happy. He has blessed the world with the restored gospel. He has opened the way for our return to the realm of glory in the life to come.

PONDERING

Loyal love radiates in the lives of faithful sons and daughters of the Lord. We can all do a little better each day in showing our loyalty and love for the Savior and His children. As you seek to improve these qualities in your own life, please consider the following questions:

• In what ways have devoted women of your acquaintance or in your family lineage shown memorable qualities of loyalty and love that you can emulate?

• What guidance has come to you as you have prayed for strength to overcome hindrances and manifest more loyal love to the Lord and His sons and daughters?

• In what ways does the radiant example of Ruth empower you to help others turn to the Lord for guidance and strength to overcome tribulation?

• What feelings have come to you in reaching out to individuals and families from other cultures by inviting them to learn more about the restored gospel of Jesus Christ? How can you do so with more success in the future?

• How have you felt peace and tranquility in living the gospel and worshipping the Lord "in spirit and in truth" (JST John 4:26)?

• When you think of the "living water" spoken of by Jesus in His discussion with the Samaritan woman at the well, what comforting thoughts come to your mind? How can we all partake more fully of this living water?

CHAPTER THREE

Abundant Sharing

*For this child I prayed; and the Lord hath given me my
petition which I asked of him: Therefore also I have lent him
to the Lord; as long as he liveth he shall be lent to the Lord.*
(1 Samuel 1:27–28)

THE GOSPEL OF JESUS CHRIST is anchored in sharing. As the Lord shares
with us abundant blessings of redeeming mercy, we too learn to share with
others our love and encouragement. All of us have opportunities each day
to share, lift, guide, and relieve burdens. That is a source of joy in a world
of tribulation. President Henry B. Eyring assured us that we are on the
pathway of purification when we have an increased desire to serve others
and share with them our love and help (see "Service and Eternal Life,"
Liahona, March 2014).

The greatest of all eternal gifts is the Father's sharing of His Firstborn
Son for the salvation and exaltation of all mankind. "Whom shall I send?"
asked the Father before the foundation of the world. The first to respond
in willingness was Jehovah, and the Father said, "I will send the first" (Abraham 3:27). That merciful act of divine sharing was anchored in endless love: "The Father loveth the Son, and hath given all things into his hand" (John 3:35). In turn,

> "The greatest of all eternal gifts is the Father's sharing of His Firstborn Son for the salvation and exaltation of all mankind."

the Son shared His infinite love by giving His life willingly as an act of
grace for our redemption: "As the Father hath loved me, so have I loved
you: continue ye in my love" (John 15:9). By continuing in the love of
the Savior, we have His promise of returning to His presence in glory:

"Father, I will that they also, whom thou hast given me, be with me where I am; that they may behold my glory, which thou hast given me: for thou lovedst me before the foundation of the world" (John 17:24).

Eternal womanhood partakes of the essence of divine sharing in glorious ways. Eliza R. Snow captured the warmth of that truth in the words of her hymn "O My Father" (*Hymns*, no. 292): "In the heav'ns are parents single? / No, the thought makes reason stare! / Truth is reason; truth eternal / Tells me I've a mother there." Just as our Father in Heaven shared His Son with us, so likewise did our Mother in Heaven partake of that transcendent act of benevolence. In turn, the daughters of God often demonstrate a high measure of sharing by reaching out to others with gifts of love, nurture, and gospel light.

Mothers in Zion in all generations have shared their precious children in the service of building up the kingdom of God. Since the dawning of the Restoration, over a million missionaries from the homes of Zion have traversed the earth, spreading the truths of the restored gospel. The Lord promised His Saints: "Behold, I will hasten my work in its time" (D&C 88:73). That hastening is now coming to pass through the lowering of the ages of youth called to full-time missionary service. The prayers of fathers and mothers have risen to the heavens in faithful supplication for the safety and devotion of these sons and daughters of the covenant.

1. One Moment in Eternity: Hannah

We see unfolded in the scriptures the goodness of many faithful women who radiate a sublime spirit of abundant sharing. One of these was Hannah, the mother of the prophet Samuel. Some details of her life are given in the first two chapters of the first book of Samuel. Can we sense the sensations, feelings, and yearnings that must have arisen in her heart as she prayed for the opportunity to be a mother in Zion and share her love with a child? Let us look back and imagine how it must have been as she experienced remarkable blessings from the Lord in overcoming a troubling burden that had encompassed her for many years.

> She paused and knelt to admire a lonely wild plant growing along the pathway leading away from the house of the Lord. Tenderly, she plucked from the plant a tiny bouquet of fragrant purple blossoms and clutched them gently in her fingers. The cool morning breeze brushed the locks of hair away from before her eyes as she rose once again to watch a woman and two young

girls approaching arm-in-arm through the shadows of a distant grove of olive trees. The faint melody of a song they were singing stroked her spirit with the harmony of love and fondness.

She sighed as memories seemed to awaken inside her. Over the years, the sight of children had aroused within her a blending of emotions—deep yearning as well as sublime joy. In the past, her yearning had grown more profound with her continuing anxiety about her inability to bear children. At the same time, she had fostered feelings of joy for the women around her who were immersed in the glow of motherhood. She had been inspired with their motherly compassion of holding their children forever close. She had been warmed in her heart with their affection and nurture.

But her loneliness and emptiness while watching others nurture their children had generated within her a never-ending tearful plea unto God for the miracle of recovery. Now, with the dawn edging over the horizon, she recalled those bleak times and rehearsed within her soul the words of her unfolding prayer: "O Lord of hosts, if thou wilt indeed look on the affliction of thine handmaid, and remember me, and not forget thine handmaid, but wilt give unto thine handmaid a man child, then I will give him unto the Lord all the days of his life."[64] And smiling in gratitude, she whispered thanks to the Lord that her prayer had indeed been answered.

Just then the mother and her two young daughters reached the spot where Hannah was standing, immersed in soulful reminiscence. They smiled at her with friendly countenances.

"How beautiful are your daughters," she said pleasantly to the mother, handing to each of the girls a purple blossom. "You are blossoms from the Lord, and your mother is a tender gardener from heaven." They nodded warmly and continued on their way.

She turned to watch them fade into the distance as the rising sun sent beams of light climbing over the walls of the house of the Lord where the ark of the covenant was preserved. "Thank you, Lord," she whispered. "You have transformed my yearnings into everlasting gratitude. My Samuel is a gift from heaven."

Wiping a tear of joy from her eye, she clutched tightly against her bosom the satchel in which she had just transported a newly prepared coat for her son. Each year since the beginning of his service as a young lad in the house of the Lord, she had toiled to weave cloth from threads of love and bind the fabric with gentleness into a handsome cloak in support of his unfolding ministry. How pleased he had been to receive the mantle of motherly compassion earlier this morning. How joyful she had been to embrace him with motherly affection on yet another visit as part of this pattern of journeying from Ramah "with her husband to offer the yearly sacrifice."[65]

She looked peacefully toward the house of the Lord with a feeling of deep satisfaction. The coat had been her offering this day, but she knew there was a greater offering to celebrate, for in honor and obedience to her vow she had offered unto the Lord her greatest treasure, even her firstborn son. The words of her promise echoed once again within the chambers of her heart at that moment: "For this child I prayed; and the Lord hath given me my petition which I asked of him: Therefore also I have lent him to the Lord; as long as he liveth he shall be lent to the Lord."[66]

Just then she felt a hand slip gently into her own. Coming up from behind, her husband, Elkanah, now looked down into her eyes and smiled a silent confirmation of his love for her. He held her closely and whispered softly into her ear words to the effect, "Just as you have clothed our son each year with a coat of maternal protection, so the Lord is clothing him eternally in the fatherly mantle of prophetic authority."

She nodded and whispered back, "We were wise to name him Samuel, for he truly is the 'name of God.'"

Her husband responded with words of quiet bless, "I will never forget your words of prayerful praise unto the Lord when He blessed us with this son: 'There is none holy as the Lord: for there is none beside thee: neither is there any rock like our God.'"[67]

With a glow in her eye, she replied, "And I will never forget the next words that flowed into my heart on that occasion through the Spirit of the Lord: 'The Lord shall judge the ends of the earth; and he shall give strength unto his king, and exalt the horn of his anointed.'"[68]

Her husband leaned over and gave her a kiss. "Our Samuel," he said, "will guide our people down the pathway toward our heavenly king." Then, hand-in-hand, in the spirit of peace, they started walking together on a journey homeward.

In the abundance of motherhood, Hannah was blessed thereafter with five more children, three sons and two daughters (see 1 Samuel 2:21).

In maternal fondness, Hannah watched her son Samuel grow in stature as he "ministered before the Lord" (1 Samuel 2:18). He rose as one of the Lord's greatest prophets. His life and ministry partook of the love and grace of his mother, one of the choicest of the righteous and valiant women celebrated in the scriptures. Little did she know at the time that her words of inspired praise, promising that God would "exalt the horn [i.e., power] of his anointed" (1 Samuel 2:10), would serve as a milestone of scriptural pronouncement. In her humility and sacred service, she did not realize that her chosen word *anointed* would one day be regarded as the earliest pronouncement of the equivalent of *Messiah* in all generations. Her abundant sharing of her own son is an emblem of how the Father shared His Only Begotten Son as an eternal blessing for the salvation and exaltation of the sons and daughters of God.

2. SISTERLY ECHOES: ELISABETH

The spirit of sharing is mirrored in countless lives through the generations, including the contribution of Elisabeth as the mother of John the Baptist, nearly a millennium after the time of Hannah. When a woman of the Lord waits years to receive a blessed child, what thoughts and feelings might well stir within her being as she ponders the future? The ideas expressed in the first chapter of the Gospel of Luke provide a framework for the following scene:

> Time alone with an angel child! Elisabeth could scarcely endure the transforming burning in her bosom. She held the tiny infant in her arms and experienced the enduring miracle of oneness with a new life—scarcely eight days old.[69] Knowing that her neighbors and relatives would soon arrive to share with her the bliss of the occasion, she savored the peace flooding through the silent room and commenced a quiet, motherly dialogue in the dawning light of the early morning.
>
> The infant was looking up into her eyes with a light of infinite penetration. "You are the answer to our prayers," she said.[70] "You have blessed an aging woman with the ecstasy of motherhood."

The babe wiggled as if caressed with the energy of her words. "How I rejoiced during the visit of my cousin Mary when you 'leaped in [my] womb; and [I] was filled with the Holy Ghost.'[71] You were blessed in the same manner, just as the holy visitor from heaven promised your father concerning you: 'For he shall be great in the sight of the Lord, . . . and he shall be filled with the Holy Ghost, even from his mother's womb.'"[72]

Elisabeth looked down into the child's eyes and perceived through the searching imagination of her mind a reflection of the soothing eyes of the Lord Himself. "He too 'looked on me, to take away my reproach,'"[73] she uttered, thinking of the lonely years of her bareness. "You are the blessed joy of heaven in my life. Thank you, Lord. Thank you, child. 'For with God nothing shall be impossible.'"[74]

A tiny hand clutched her finger as she gently stroked his feet with her other hand. "These hands and feet will do mighty miracles," she said to the babe. "It is just as the angel proclaimed: "And many of the children of Israel shall [you] turn to the Lord their God. And [you] shall go before him . . . to make ready a people prepared for the Lord.'"[75]

The sound of cheerful conversation from the nearby hills of the Judean countryside announced the imminent arrival of guests. The babe emitted a noise of reaction. "Fear not," Elisabeth whispered, "for as the heavens proclaimed, 'many shall rejoice at [your] birth.'"[76]

With that, several gracious guests from the surrounding hillside entered the room and were immediately reduced to awestruck silence at the magnificent scene of maternal glory displayed before them. They inched closer to the mother and child and whispered marveling gasps of joy for the miracle presented to their eyes.

Elisabeth felt the love of her neighbors. "Thank you for showing great mercy upon me and rejoicing with me."[77]

One onlooker leaned back toward the child's father, who had guided them into the room, to confirm that the child would be given the same name as his father, Zacharias.

The mother smiled and shook her head. "Not so; but he shall be called John."[78]

The group was surprised by that announcement, saying to her, "There is none of thy kindred that is called by this name."[79] With questioning looks, they turned toward the husband for further enlightenment.

Since his capacity to speak had been suspended following his visit with the angel in the temple nine months earlier, he motioned for a writing tablet and wrote the words, "His name is John," causing all to marvel.[80]

Instantly another miracle occurred—this time with the father: "And his mouth was opened immediately, and his tongue *loosed*, and he spake, and praised God."[81] The room was filled with the light of the Holy Ghost as his words of prophecy ensued in buoyant power to lift all within the circle. Elisabeth was filled with rapture to hear again a confirmation of the divine ministry of this tiny babe:

And thou, child, shalt be called the prophet of the Highest: for thou shalt go before the face of the Lord to prepare his ways;

To give knowledge of salvation unto his people by the remission of their sins,

Through the tender mercy of our God; whereby the dayspring from on high hath visited us,

To give light to them that sit in darkness and in the shadow of death, to guide our feet into the way of peace.[82]

In the months and years to follow, "the child grew, and waxed strong in spirit, and was in the deserts till the day of his shewing unto Israel" (Luke 1:80). Both mother and father contributed to the unfolding of his holy ministry, for both were "righteous before God, walking in all the commandments and ordinances of the Lord blameless" (Luke 1:6). From them we can take into our hearts an inspiring example of pure devotion. And from Elisabeth, in special measure, we can savor the spirit of abundant sharing as she fulfilled her calling of eternal motherhood by offering this choice son to the Lord as the one chosen to prepare the way for His redeeming mission. She is, therefore, a sisterly echo of the offering of Hannah and a further model of an authentic spirit of willing oblation.

3. A Modern Moment: A Willing Heart

From the seeds of faith spring forth sprouts destined to unfold as trees of everlasting life. The gift of eternal womanhood rises and matures in the same manner, nurtured and sustained by the Spirit of the Lord. Acts of gracious sharing along the way manifest the process of developing enduring and authentic charity, as the following true account from a member of a stake presidency demonstrates:

A pure and warming spirit followed her into our home. From her eyes beamed the light of youthful radiance. Her smile was evidence of joy and friendliness.

We welcomed her into our living room and listened intently as she spoke of her family background and expressed her deep interest in the Church. Her words soon confirmed that the recommendation of a former stake president to invite

> " Acts of gracious sharing along the way manifest the process of developing enduring and authentic charity "

her to our home was an inspired idea. Here was a choice daughter of destiny who reflected a yearning for spiritual truth.

As we discussed the basic principles of the gospel together, she raised a question that had been hovering in her mind. My wife and I listened intently as she put the inquiry into heartfelt words: "Do the Mormons pay tithing?"

"Yes," I responded. "What is your understanding of that principle?"

Without hesitation, she replied with an expression of sincerity, "I understand that tithing means paying one-third of my income to the Lord."

Somewhat surprised, I asked her, "Would you be willing to pay that much to the Lord?"

"Certainly," she replied, with a most sincere and warm spirit about her.

I then explained to her what the Lord asks of His Saints in Section 119 of the Doctrine and Covenants, verse 4—that they would "pay one-tenth of all their interest annually." I bore my testimony to her that such devoted service will result in immeasurable blessings of the type promised through the prophet Malachi: "Prove me now herewith, saith the Lord of hosts, if I will not open you the windows of heaven, and pour you out a blessing, that there shall not be room enough to receive it."[83]

Her eyes were still bright and her smile still radiant as she savored even more deeply the essence of the spiritual principle of sharing. My heart was touched by her spirit. My wife and I complimented her on her humble devotion and willingness to do whatever the Lord would ask of her. I perceived through the Spirit that she was truly a sharing convert, and I knew with certainty that the Lord would grant her sublime blessings for her devotion and service.

This young woman soon joined the Church and rendered much service in the spirit of humility and obedience. To this day, my wife and I remain impressed with her angelic faith and acceptance of the will of the Lord. She exemplifies the principle taught by the Lord: "Verily I say unto you, all among them who know their hearts are honest, and are broken, and their spirits contrite, and are willing to observe their covenants by sacrifice— yea, every sacrifice which I, the Lord, shall command—they are accepted of me."[84]

This young woman was and is a daughter of destiny who nurtured from her earliest years the seeds of faith and sharing, seeds that sprouted and grew over time into a blossoming tree of spiritual strength, bearing the fruit of love and glory. Abundant sharing unfolded with radiance in her life as she nurtured and cultivated the light of eternal womanhood. All of the sons and daughters of the Lord can benefit from such examples, models of righteous choosing and enduring devotion.

PONDERING

As you seek the Lord's help in developing in your own life a higher measure of righteous sharing, please consider the following questions:

- What women from your lineage or circle of friends have been inspiring examples of abundant sharing? How have they manifested a fullness of the spirit of giving, sharing, nurturing, and sustaining?

- The Father gave His Son—and the Son, His life—for our salvation. How can you more fully follow in Their footsteps through abundant offering of time, talents, and resources—even in the service of your own children—to help advance the cause of Zion?

- In what ways can the mothers of today—in the spirit of Hannah and Elisabeth—"lend" their sons and daughters to the Lord for the building up of the kingdom of God on earth?

- In what ways has the Lord guided you to share more with others and lift their spirits? How might His guidance help you overcome your own sense of inadequacy?

- How does the Holy Ghost enhance your commitment to serve the Lord and offer your most precious resources in support of His gospel plan?

- In what ways does your conviction that "with God nothing shall be impossible" (Luke 1:37) help you magnify your commitment to consecrate your life to the Lord?

- In what ways have you personally felt the living seeds of "sharing" unfold within you as you do your best to follow the Lord in obedience?

CHAPTER FOUR

Eternal Light

But the Lord shall be unto thee an everlasting light, and thy
God thy glory. (Isaiah 60:19)

A KEY MISSION OF ETERNAL womanhood is to rise as the fount of light and radiance in this world of challenge. Where does that glorious mission originate? With our Father in Heaven. He is the God of light. He has "a crown of eternal light upon his head" (Abraham Facsimile 2, Fig. 3). He unfolded the Creation with the words "Let there be light" (Genesis 1:3; Moses 2:3; Abraham 4:3). His Son magnified that light through His own atoning mission for the salvation of mankind: "I am the light of the world: he that followeth me shall not walk in darkness, but shall have the light of life" (John 8:12). Furthermore, "I am the true light that lighteth every man that cometh into the world" (D&C 93:2; see also D&C 88:11, 13).

Because the Savior is our direct and abiding source of enduring light, we can, in turn, serve as agents of that same blessing for others: "For God, who commanded the light to shine out of darkness, hath shined in our hearts, to give the light of the knowledge of the glory of God in the face of Jesus Christ" (2 Corinthians 4:6).

In a unique and wonderful way, the daughters of Zion serve as ministering mediators of light, for they bring life into the world as mothers and serve to sustain life through nurturing love. The beacon of eternal womanhood glows with unfailing power in the shadows of our mortal journey. In the glorious future city of Zion, there will be no need for sun or moon or stars, "for the glory of God [will] lighten it, and the Lamb is the light thereof" (Revelation 21:23). The daughters of Zion look forward with courage to that celestial glory, for they aspire to illuminate their earthly homes with love and buoyant energy—whether as mothers or as nurturers of those in need.

In gratitude, we can perceive that the mission of eternal womanhood is one of rendering light and life, radiance and vitality, as the following scenes will attempt to confirm:

1. ONE MOMENT IN ETERNITY: EVE

In his 1918 vision of the spirit world, President Joseph F. Smith was able to view many of the Lord's leaders serving in that realm, including "our glorious Mother Eve, with many of her faithful daughters who had lived through the ages and worshiped the true and living God" (D&C 138:39). Let us imagine the thoughts and feelings of Eve, the first woman to embark on the mortal pathway as "the mother of all living" (Genesis 3:20; Moses 4:26):

> Slowly, silently, the features of the dark and lonely world began to emerge around her from the shadows of night, reborn in the emerging radiance of the coming day. Eve might have viewed the stark pattern of her current place of abode: a wilderness of wild brush and knotty trees, a vast enclave of open fields struggling to foster and nurture growth, a habitat for creatures sniffing for prey. She peered across the foreboding landscape toward the tops of the distant hills where the sun would soon rise in the glory of morn to deliver sweat to her brow as she continued her daily toil.
>
> Eve could not help but recall her place of origin, a place where she had been surrounded by the most beautiful garden. She knew with perfect certainty that she, like her husband, Adam, was created by God: "In the image of his own body, male and female, created he them, and blessed them, and . . . they . . . became living souls in the land upon the footstool of God."[85] Eve displayed the courage to leave that glorious garden and work alongside her husband as the mother of all living.[86]
>
> She quietly asked herself, "How many years has it been since we took leave of the Garden of Eden—that garden of delight?" Soothing memories of that glorious abode kindled a flame within her soul. What a beautiful place that was—so plush with vibrant growth; so comforting as a welcome shelter to protect against invading winds; so devoid of care and anxiety about how to sustain life; and, above all, so enriching through the visits of the Father

and the Son—Creators of this earthly realm—who shared the consoling truth about the goodness of life and the promise of the eternal family.

The warmth of those memories streamed outwardly from her heart and into the morning landscape around her, transforming the bleakness of this new world into a realm not devoid of promise and hope. Was it not promise and hope that had encompassed her being within the garden when the moment of decision rested upon her? Was it not promise and hope that had energized her vision of how she, as the mother of all living, could step forward to open the door of eternal womanhood and motherhood? Was it not promise and hope that had confirmed the wisdom of her choice to partake of the fruit and, with her husband, embark on the glorious journey of founding families destined for immortality and eternal life?

"I can still feel the flame within me," she whispered. In humility she thought of her former words: "Were it not for our transgression we never should have had seed, and never should have known good and evil, and the joy of our redemption, and the eternal life which God giveth unto all the obedient."[87]

Eve knelt down on the dew-moistened earth in a prayerful attitude. She gathered up gnarled sticks of wood, one at a time, to use in heating the coming meal for her hungering family. She placed the wood in a leather cloth nestled in her arms. *Why this toil?* she thought. But she knew and answered aloud, "Because the Lord directed us to eat our bread by the sweat of our brow. It is an honor to labor with my husband for the nurture of our children."[88]

In that instant, she felt an intense pain in one of her fingers, causing her to spring to her feet in shock. Tiny drops of blood oozed from the spot where a thorn in one of the gathered sticks had punctured her skin and left a stinging reminder of the perils of the dreary and dangerous world around her.

She sighed and shook off the discomfort by remembering the promise of the Lord: "Our sufferings, our pain, our exhaustion— all will be lifted from off our shoulders by the Redeemer, who suffers infinite pain for our redemption."

She gratefully applied in her mind the spiritual remedy of divine healing prescribed by the Lord. What were the words that had flowed to them over the walls of the distant garden? "And he gave unto them commandments, that they should worship the Lord their God, and should offer the firstlings of their flocks, for an offering unto the Lord."[89] The angel of the Lord later explained the meaning and purpose for such an offering: "This thing is a similitude of the sacrifice of the Only Begotten of the Father, which is full of grace and truth."[90]

Eve also knew that sacrifice was part of our mortal experience as sons and daughter of God. She plucked a yellow petal from a delicate spring flower and placed it gently on her finger to wipe away the drops of blood. Then she wrapped a soothing leaf around the injury and closed her fist. *How many times have I dressed the wounds of my children in their times of injury? The Lord told me, 'I will greatly multiply thy sorrow and thy conception; in sorrow thou shalt bring forth children.'*[91] *And so it is,* she thought. *And yet what joy blossoms forth from the love we share as a family.*

Yes, this new world required sacrifice and continual effort. A mother brings forth new souls with sorrow and anguish. Parents labor without ceasing to nurture and teach their children. With bliss, Eve rehearsed in her mind how she and her husband, from the very beginning of their mortal journey, had "blessed the name of God, and they made all things known unto their sons and their daughters."[92]

Eve suddenly felt the touch of a hand on her shoulder. She looked up with a start and caught sight of her husband in the emerging light. He smiled as he reached out and handed her a blossom from an apple tree they had been cultivating—yes, an apple tree! She beamed and took in the fragrance of the fresh petals.

"Spring," she said.

He smiled and put his arm around her in loving affection while pointing toward the horizon, where a new day was about to begin. "Let it start," he said. "Let us continue to labor together for our family."

In that moment, Eve's gestures confirmed that a renewed spirit of calm and serenity was descending upon her. The Almighty was continuing to bless their lives. Hope was transforming their toil into a harvest of joy. Faith was unfolding their vision of the eternities that lay ahead. They savored peace in their hearts as the sun rose silently over the horizon—the dawning of a perfect day.

Eve is a glowing beacon of light—the light of courage, obedience, sacrifice, and love. She illuminates the journey for all the daughters of destiny—and for all mankind. Her nobility penetrates the shadows of this lonely and dreary world and reaches forward to the glory of a better home, the home of the glory of God. The sons and daughters of destiny following in her footsteps can help keep that beacon burning for the good of all mankind.

2. SISTERLY ECHOES: ABIGAIL

Down through time, the light of eternal womanhood has continued to shine forth in a world of shadows and darkness. Often the wisdom of womanly choices opens channels of liberation and illuminates the pathway of safety. The story of Abigail, summarized in chapter 25 of the first book of Samuel, shows how a woman of courage made a vital decision that saved her community from destruction and ignited the light of harmony at a time of great contention. Let us construct in our imagination a view of the events surrounding Abigail's actions and aspire to grasp a clearer understanding of the qualities that made her a victor on the landscape of mortality.

Undaunted by the alarming scene emerging ahead of her, Abigail accelerated her pace along the pathway leading upward into the foothills above Carmel. But the servants and maidens in her company began to slow their forward motion as a massive company of warriors stampeded into clearer view, surging down the distant hillside, sending ominous clouds of dust rising into the sky.

"Move forward!" Abigail counseled her companions with a firm voice. "They hope to bring darkness and death—yet we hope to bring light and life!"

"But mistress," responded one of her helpers, "they are raising their swords toward us!"

At that moment the reflection of the midday sun from hundreds of blades of terror sent blinding flashes across the terrain as the approaching army closed the gap between the two groups.

A flock of birds suddenly burst from the surrounding brush and escaped into the air. A lonely coyote howled in terror and fled off into the distance.

Still undaunted, Abigail held her head high and continued approaching the descending warriors, now thundering toward her with threatening shouts of warning and power.

She was about to confront a wave of immense power bent on taking the lives of all the individuals in her community—especially that of her husband, Nabal. It was Nabal who had ungraciously denied the request of these warriors for food and supplies to survive the murderous conspiracies of King Saul. Would Abigail be able to succeed in her mission to reverse the militia's campaign, now within shouting distance of her company?

As she continued speedily on her way, she focused her view on the leader of the band. His shield reflected the glint of the sun. His countenance emitted a look of irreversible commitment to victory. His locks rose and fell rhythmically with the pace of his unrelenting motion. His eyes began to penetrate into the face of the woman leading her company of maidens and servants toward him with an endless column of pack-animals loaded with—

"What is this," he seemed to wonder. "Food and supplies?"

The commander slowed his pace and raised a hand to bring the army to a stop. He was confronted with an unprecedented and miraculous opportunity to transform his plan. It was David, the one anointed by the Lord to become the king of Judah and Israel. On her own initiative, Abigail was acting to sustain the lives of his hungering troop.

Abigail came before David, amazed him by falling down at his feet in pure humility, and then rose up again in majesty to use words of power designed to displace the spirit of revenge with forgiveness, of fury with nobility, and of anger with compassion.

"Upon me, my lord," she said, "upon me let this iniquity be."[93] Abigail was taking upon herself all responsibility for the folly and disrespect shown by her husband. She promised David that if he would abandon his plot of revenge, the Lord would make of him "a sure house; because my lord fighteth the battles of the Lord, and evil hath not been found in thee all thy days."[94] If he would rise in honor this day, "the soul of my lord shall be bound in the bundle of life with the Lord thy God; and the souls of thine enemies, them shall he sling out, as out of the middle of a sling."[95] David would thus fulfill his divine destiny to become "ruler over Israel."[96]

She concluded her astounding presentation with the words, "But when the Lord shall have dealt well with my lord, then remember thine handmaid."[97] It was one brief moment when the spirit of eternal womanhood once again brought light into the shadows of mortal gloominess.

Her presentation mesmerized David. He suspended his planned campaign against Nabal and declared, "Blessed be the Lord God of Israel, which sent thee this day to meet me: And blessed be thy advice, and blessed be thou, which hast kept me this day from coming to shed blood, and from avenging myself with mine own hand."[98]

Soon thereafter, Nabal would pass away. When David learned of his passing, he sent for Abigail, who accepted his proposal for marriage.

Abigail means "source of rejoicing." Her enlightened courage preserved joy in the face of sorrow and brought light into the lives of many. She was "a woman of good understanding, and of a beautiful countenance" (1 Samuel 25:3). Even more important, her *spiritual* beauty and noble character prevailed over the threatening clouds of darkness rising around her—especially those reflected in the life of her husband Nabal, a name meaning "foolish" or "villainous."

Through the light of inspiration, Abigail dispersed the threat of chaos and destruction in her own lonely and dreary world. She saved her people. Like the Savior, she reached out in the spirit of compassion and preserved her community in the face of death. Like Eve, she is a beacon of light. She is a sisterly echo of the faithfulness of the many daughters of destiny who have worshipped and honored "the true and living God" (D&C 138:39). Her spirit, like the spirit of Eve, still manifests itself in the lives of countless women in our day, who, despite weaknesses and trials, rise in the strength of the Lord to overcome the challenges of mortality and keep the beacon of light burning brightly.

3. A MODERN MOMENT: LIGHTING THE CANDLE OF HOPE

How do the exemplary qualities of Eve, Abigail, and other daughters of destiny inspire you to find light and truth in this lonely and dreary world? How have you been able to find joy in the shadows of life and share compassion and encouragement with all of those around you? Consider the following true account and its symbolic possibilities:

Another Wednesday, so late in the evening. Rose—we'll call her by that name—stared at the red light above the deserted intersection, beaming crimson fear into her lonely heart. She was gripping the steering wheel with white-knuckled hands and taking short, panting breaths like a prisoner held captive by the towering elm trees standing as eerie sentinels on all sides of the street.

Would the light turn green soon enough to let her escape before the approaching car reached her and discovered a lonely woman stopped there? Would her aging car suffer another breakdown—as it had one evening on the university campus—leaving her abandoned until her husband could speed across the vast metropolis to her side for a late-night rescue?

Rose uttered a sigh of relief as the light turned green, and she raced through the night on the journey to reach home and greet her family in the spirit of warmth and safety. Her thoughts confirmed the pattern: Every Wednesday evening was the same—singing all the way down to campus and shivering all the way back. Then happiness again to arrive home that evening—the only evening of the week when her husband was free from his work to watch their children.

She had relived the pattern each week for five long years. Week by week, darkness was turned into light, loneliness was supplanted by togetherness, dreariness was transformed into energy to continue her studies in the quest to become a more knowledgeable mother and wife. As she worked to complete her college degree, she pondered frequently the counsel of the Lord: "Seek ye out of the best books words of wisdom; seek learning, even by study and also by faith."[99] She pressed forward "with a steadfastness in Christ, having a perfect brightness of hope, and a love of God and of all men."[100] Her dream was to endure to the end and help her family receive the blessings of heaven, "even peace in this world and eternal life in the world to come."[101]

"There are always challenges to overcome, weakness to transform into strengths, goals to achieve with resolve and courage. But in the strength of the Lord, such women keep the light of wellness and gospel vitality ablaze."

Here was a woman, a daughter of destiny, who was choosing to labor in faith to overcome the challenges of life and become a beacon of light and hope in a shadowy world. She was moved by a vision of faith, a vision to learn how to care for her children with enduring compassion and wisdom. She manifested the spirit of love characteristic of all the daughters of God who carry on their family and community service with devotion. Yes, there are always challenges to overcome, weakness to transform into strengths, goals to achieve with resolve and courage. But in the strength of the Lord, such women keep the light of wellness and gospel vitality ablaze. They stand as beacons of light and ensigns of glory.

PONDERING

For each of us, life can be a mixture of shadows and light, disappointments and joy. But through the blessings of the Lord and the guidance of the Spirit, we can keep the light of obedience and service burning brightly. Please ponder the following questions as you explore ways to improve your commitment of faithfulness and gratitude before the Lord:

- Which qualities of Eve, Abigail, and their exemplary successors of our day stand out as beacons of light for you?

- How might their wisdom and courage inspire you to serve the Lord and help build His kingdom with greater resolve?

- What influences of darkness lurk in the shadows of our modern culture, and what means can you use to dispel such influences with the light of the Lord and the power of His gospel plan?

- How can the sacrifice of a broken heart and a contrite spirit ignite within your life the flame of hope and the fire of covenant loyalty? How can this flame contribute to your identity as a son or daughter of God, renewed and rejuvenated through obedience to the principles and covenants of the gospel?

- Have you felt the glow of comfort and peace as you have lived the gospel? Are there ways you could savor the light of the gospel more fully?

- How can you better serve as an example of light for your loved ones and all who are seeking the way to salvation and exaltation?

CHAPTER FIVE

Noble Leadership

For the Lamb which is in the midst of the throne shall feed
them, and shall lead them unto living fountains of waters: and
God shall wipe away all tears from their eyes. (Revelation 7:17)

THE GREATEST GIFT OF LEADERSHIP flows to us through the service and
sacrifice of the Savior. He taught the simple truth: "But he that is greatest
among you shall be your servant" (Matthew 23:11). He reaches out to
each one of us with a sacred promise: "Be thou humble; and the Lord
thy God shall lead thee by the hand, and give thee answer to thy prayers"
(D&C 112:10). Through His divine leadership, He opens the windows of
inspiration to give us certainty about how to move forward in faith along
the pathway of life and salvation: "And now, verily, verily, I say unto thee,
put your trust in that Spirit which leadeth to do good—yea, to do justly,
to walk humbly, to judge righteously; and this is my Spirit" (D&C 11:12).
He gives us light "to go by day and night" (Exodus 13:21), saying, "And I
will bring the blind by a way that they knew not; I will lead them in paths
that they have not known: I will make darkness light before them, and
crooked things straight. These things will I do unto them, and not forsake
them" (Isaiah 42:16).

For each of us—each man, woman, and child in the family of God—
the Savior is the eternal example of leadership. He shows us how to gain
a firm and solid foundation in a world of uncertainty and fading values:
"And if my people will hearken unto my voice, and unto the voice of my
servants whom I have appointed to lead my people, behold, verily I say
unto you, they shall not be moved out of their place" (D&C 124:45). He
encourages us to "be of good cheer, for I will lead you along. The kingdom
is yours and the blessings thereof are yours, and the riches of eternity are
yours" (D&C 78:18).

In a special way, the spirit of eternal womanhood partakes of the Savior's light of leadership, for the daughters of the Lord apply His example in faith as they open the channels of life, lead families, plant seeds of growth, nurture celestial qualities in loved ones, and show the way of goodness through their courage and example. The history of God's people contains vibrant examples of how the women of the Lord rise as leaders who serve with valor in bringing forth His kingdom and blessing the lives of His children.

1. ONE MOMENT IN ETERNITY: ESTHER

What can we do in the spirit of righteous leadership to help bring deliverance and joy to our loved ones and to all those who seek the gospel of truth? The story of Esther (meaning "star") is one of great courage and faith. The details of her memorable life are given in the book of Esther, one of the late historical books of the Old Testament (along with Ezra and Nehemiah). The events in the book of Esther occurred some half century following the return of many Jewish captives from Babylon, as authorized by the decree of Cyrus in 537 BC. Esther emerges as the paragon of fearless leadership by securing the liberation of her people.

Let us view in our mind's eye how she must have felt and thought and acted in accordance with the inspiration of the Lord to achieve her appointed assignment.

> Her head high in keeping with the stately nobility of her mission, Esther offered a silent prayer to the Lord as she waited solemnly in the courtyard outside the closed door leading to the throne room of her husband, the king. She understood clearly the rule of law: to open the door unannounced and enter as an unscheduled visitor would be considered sedition and could result in death.
>
> She perfectly grasped the perilous risk, but she knew that the preservation of her Jewish compatriots throughout the realm was at stake—their extermination having been ordered by the conspiracy of Haman, chief officer serving under the king. She sensed the critical importance of her position as deliverer, the only one who might be able to intercede on behalf of every man, woman, and child of Jewish descent in the land. She pondered silently what her cousin and adoptive father Mordecai had told her in recent days: "Who knoweth whether thou art come to the kingdom for such a time as this?"[102]

The thought that her calling came of the Lord refreshed her resolve and brought her soul a feeling of tranquility. Therefore—despite the peril—she reached toward the handle of the door. "Am I not come into the kingdom for this very purpose? If I turn back, thousands will disappear from the face of the earth under the hand of evil."

She pondered in her heart the faith of her people, who had obediently followed the words of her recent counsel: "Go, gather together all the Jews that are present in Shushan, and fast ye for me, and neither eat nor drink three days, night or day: I also and my maidens will fast likewise; and so will I go in unto the king, which *is* not according to the law: and if I perish, I perish."[103]

She sensed in her heart their sweet glow of hope as she took the handle in a firm grip, knowing the hazards of her act. If the king would listen and respond with wisdom, a milestone in history would be passed, and her people would be saved amidst outpourings of joy and gratitude. But unless, in this very moment, the king should "hold out the golden sceptre"[104] as a signal to preserve her life, she would be executed for breaking the law.

Slowly, with dedication and faith, she turned the handle and opened the door to reveal a view of the king seated on his palatial throne among the statesmen of the court. Becoming aware of the unscheduled visitor, the king turned directly toward her and stared into her countenance for what seemed an endless length of time without any change of his expression. Her heart began to increase in its vibrant rhythm as she awaited his response. Would he . . . ?

Then he smiled at her and held forth the golden scepter as a cordial gesture, directing her to advance and be received in dignity. Immediately a spirit of utter calmness and peace unfolded within her being, for she knew that her mission for the salvation of her people would succeed. The Lord had lifted her up as an instrument of faith and deliverance. At that moment, something must have whispered in her soul words to the effect, "What is noble and right, what is brought forth by courage and honor, what is according to the eternal design of the Lord—that is what comes to pass in this life and in the eternities."

Esther, who from the beginning had obtained grace and favor in the sight of King Ahasuerus, her husband,[105] prevailed upon him to suspend the extermination decree against her people. The king then ordered Haman hanged on the very gallows that the chief officer had secretly erected for hanging Mordecai. Mordecai was subsequently elevated to Haman's position at court, second only to the king.[106] The outcome was a blessing from heaven to be celebrated by the Jewish people for generations to come. Because of her noble leadership, "The Jews had light, and gladness, and joy, and honour."[107]

The story of Esther is one of great courage, faith, and leadership. In the same way, our own acts of courage may well be the fulfillment of a destined role of leadership that is part of our own calling. In today's world there is a special need for us all to rise fearless and firm in our resolve to support the cause of truth and righteousness. This is especially true of the women of Zion who serve as leaders in the forward march of the Lord's people. Some might suppose that, as queen, Esther had special advantages to sustain her mission, yet we can find comfort in the counsel of Patricia T. Holland and Jeffrey R. Holland as they discuss the contributions of Esther, Ruth, and other role models, each with different stations and abilities. The Hollands confirm that the Lord calls us to serve *because* of our different personalities and unique qualities rather than *in spite* of them. The Lord needs

" Manifesting the nobility of character to do what one knows is right requires the integrity of the soul. "

of all us—with all of our limitations and imperfections (see *On Earth As It Is in Heaven* [Salt Lake City: Deseret Book, 1989], p. 8).

There are challenges to overcome and decisions to be made. None of us is perfect, but through the guidance of the Holy Ghost, we can serve in the spirit of deliverance for those we love. Manifesting the nobility of character to do what one knows is right requires the integrity of the soul. Like Esther, we can all be more courageous in standing up for our beliefs and values, knowing that "in the strength of the Lord [we can] do all things" (Alma 20:4).

2. SISTERLY ECHOES: DEBORAH

The following scene about the leadership of Deborah, one of the righteous judges in Israel, confirms the verity of the principle that "with God nothing shall be impossible" (Luke 1:37). What we know of Deborah is preserved in chapters 4 and 5 of the book of Judges. Let us join with her as silent observers of her remarkable leadership and come to understand more fully the significance of her decisions and service on behalf of the Lord's people.

"Will you go with us or not?"

That question from her military associate Barak penetrated the silence of the mountain air and flowed smoothly into her heart, where the nestling answer had been unfolding and maturing for no fewer than twenty years. The two of them were now facing one another beneath the sheltering shade of the palms on an elevated plateau. In that very spot, she had been listening for years with heartfelt compassion to similar questions from an endless stream of God's people burdened with anxiety, stoked by the merciless encroachments of their Canaanite enemies.

"Will you join with us to find relief?" they would ask the prophetess[108] and mother in Israel.[109] "Will you pray unto God that He might deliver us from suffering?" they had begged her continually. "Will you come down into our homes and bring a blessing for our children who are hungry and ailing?"

Her response to them had been forever the same, with words to the effect, "Will *you* follow the Lord's laws and move forward along the pathway of salvation?"

Feelings of compassion as well as courage rose within her soul. A warm breeze from the south brushed across her face. She smiled and looked upward into the sky above her, welcoming the vista of wispy clouds floating gently over the hills.

At that moment Deborah must have sensed the warming relief in her soul to be so gently reminded by Mother Nature that unstoppable blessings can flow from the Lord of mercy. She glanced toward the north, shivering for a moment at the sight of the darkening clouds churning ominously across the distant horizon, marking the boundaries of the enemy forces gathering for a final invasion. She wondered, "Will the gentle white clouds from the south dispel the stormy darkness of the north?" She knew the answer and nodded with comfort at the assurances of the Spirit.

What had the Lord directed her to do? To send Barak, her army commander, leading ten thousand soldiers of Israel against

Sisera, the Canaanite despot, with his nine hundred chariots
of iron and vast multitude of fighters.[110] What was the Lord's
promise? "I will deliver him into thine hand."[111]

"Will you go with us or not?" Barak's words echoed in her
memory once again. She understood the sincerity of the question.
What he meant was precisely this: "If thou wilt go with me, then
I will go: but if thou wilt not go with me, then I will not go."[112]

The stakes were high. Only if the judge of Israel, Deborah
herself, would go forth at the head of the army, would the people
of the Lord know with utter certainty that the Lord's promise of
deliverance was rooted in a covenant guarantee. Courage instills
enduring hope; leadership cements inexorable certainty.

Waiting for the answer, Barak proclaimed, "Your name means
'bee.' The sting of the bee will dispel the enemy."

Deborah smiled and responded with gentleness but firmness,
"The sting comes not from me but from the Lord, who declares
the day of infamy is to end." Barak nodded with a glow in his eyes.
She continued, "Your name means 'lightning.' You will add to the
fire of heaven in this holy enterprise of deliverance."

He responded with a smile, "It is not I, but the lightning of
the Lord that will save us."

They nodded toward each other in an expression of
understanding and mutual accord.

Then she gripped his hands and confirmed what he already
knew: "I will surely go with thee."[113]

Thus was confirmed the covenant arrangement that would
save Israel from oppression—a covenant reflective of the promise
of salvation that flows from the heavens unto the faithful sons
and daughters of Zion. The commanding words of Deborah then
recaptured the power of the moment: "Up; for this is the day in
which the Lord hath delivered Sisera into thine hand: is not the
Lord gone out before thee?"[114] They arose and set off together
toward Barak's hometown of Kedesh to prepare to face the enemy
waiting in the shadows.

What ensued was the decisive battle along the river of Kishon
in the plain of Jezreel, where the forces of Israel destroyed the
enemy in the strength of the Lord and where the life of Sisera,
their cruel commander, was also brought to an end.[115]

Deborah and Barak then joined in the proclamation of a grand victory anthem that would go down in history as one of the great poetic statements of triumph in all of world literature. What do we hear in that anthem but expressions of noble leadership anchored in the guidance of the greatest Leader of the universe, the Lord Almighty:

Praise ye the Lord for the avenging of Israel, when the people willingly offered themselves.

Hear, O ye kings; give ear, O ye princes; I, even I, will sing unto the Lord; I will sing praise to the Lord God of Israel.[116]

The inhabitants of the villages ceased, they ceased in Israel, until that I Deborah arose, that I arose a mother in Israel.[117]

They that are delivered from the noise of archers in the places of drawing water, there shall they rehearse the righteous acts of the Lord, even the righteous acts toward the inhabitants of his villages in Israel: then shall the people of the Lord go down to the gates.

Awake, awake, Deborah: awake, awake, utter a song: arise, Barak, and lead thy captivity captive, thou son of Abinoam.[118]

They fought from heaven; the stars in their courses fought against Sisera.[119]

So let all thine enemies perish, O Lord: but let them that love him be as the sun when he goeth forth in his might.[120]

Deborah served as the fourth judge in the sequence of judges in Israel, from the time of Joshua to the time of Samuel—a period of several hundred years. She is celebrated as an exponent of the kind of leadership that advanced the cause of the Lord's people during an era of crisis and transition. Deborah anticipated the example of Esther, who served many hundreds of years later in the second half of the fifth century BC. Both of them have endured as exemplars of how the leadership qualities of eternal womanhood can be applied in the lives of all sons and daughters of destiny.

We all face our own personal Siseras and Hamans. Through the blessings of heaven, we can stand firm, despite our imperfections, and rise in strength according to the counsel of Nephi: "Wherefore, ye must press forward with a steadfastness in Christ, having a perfect brightness of hope, and a love of God and of all men. Wherefore, if ye shall press forward, feasting upon the word of Christ, and endure to the end, behold, thus saith the Father: Ye shall have eternal life" (2 Nephi 31:20; see also "Press Forward, Saints," *Hymns*, no. 81).

*3. A Modern Moment: Guiding the Children of God out of the
Shadows*

In every community there are individuals who reflect the nobility of
leadership that aspires to enhance the happiness of others. The following
true account about a woman of compassion—we will call her Melanie—
serves to remind us about the achievements of those who reach out to
touch lives in exceptional ways:

> Melanie strolled past a row of eager performers and reached
> for the microphone waiting atop a tall metal stand at center stage.
> In vibrant middle-age motherly tones of high-pitched enthusiasm,
> she announced to the watchful audience that a unique show was
> about to unfold. Then, one by one, she introduced each of the
> dozen or so performers by revealing to the rapt audience a special
> quality worthy of recognition in each. One of the performers
> would be singing the words of the chosen songs with a uniquely
> majestic voice. Another, she added, would be demonstrating
> unfailing skill at remembering and displaying the delicate dance
> motions for the whole team to follow. She recognized another
> as the most long-standing member of the group. Another would
> be exhibiting masterful technical skills in overseeing the controls
> of the audio system, while yet another would be an example of
> unsurpassed enthusiasm. She carried on with gusto until each
> member of the group had been hailed for goodness and skill.
>
> What she did not say was something already crystal clear to the
> audience—the obvious reason for the excitement and infectious
> smiles of the performers. What she did not put into words was
> the unifying key that blended these individuals together in a
> warm and uplifting assemblage of joyful spirits. Everyone in the
> audience knew that the team of performers consisted of men and
> women with special needs, with special disabilities, and with a
> lifelong status of mental or physical disadvantages calling for an
> unusual measure of courage and commitment.
>
> Then, as the music unfolded, the group gyrated into the
> pre-subscribed pattern and put on a sensational show to dazzle
> the audience of admiring community supporters—including, in
> some cases, the parents and relatives of the dancers.
>
> The observers enjoyed the bouncing energy and flapping-
> arms ritual of "The Chicken Dance." They savored the soaring

chords of the celebrated "YMCA" anthem. They were touched by the sweet Christian sentiments reflected in the passionate lyric hymn entitled "In This Very Room."[121]

Was the performance at a Carnegie Hall level of perfection? No. But the spirit of enthusiasm and joy was celestial in nature—unsurpassed, it would seem, in all of eternity. The dancing performers were entranced with the opportunity to exhibit their dedication to do their best, despite life's challenges. As a result, the audience was transformed with the miracle unfolding before them.

How did this miracle come about? Because of the love and devotion of the woman in charge of the dance group—a woman who had for many years volunteered her leadership and dancing skills to the cause of helping the disabled to discover and reveal their hidden abilities, helping the handicapped to display their nascent talents, and helping the lonely to find the happiness of mutual respect and encouragement.

For nearly twenty years, Melanie had been meeting for an hour each Monday evening to rehearse with a little army of hopeful men and women seeking special joy. Assisted by her supportive husband, she created an organizational movement that has blessed many hundreds of lives over time and provided her community with numerous memorable public performances—some in retirement centers, some in community chapels, some in youth conferences, and some in local college settings.

Why had she done this? For two reasons: first, her own daughter, a tall and stately young woman with an endearing and continual smile, qualified as a member of the group; and secondly, because Melanie was motivated by an overpowering desire to reach out and bless the lives of all around her. She is an exemplar of the qualities of eternal womanhood—the source of heartfelt warmth, nurture, and encouragement flowing outwardly to touch myriad lives with the spirit of compassion and hope. Thus is noble leadership personified—lifting lives and warming hearts, planting seeds of hope, and harvesting the fruit of mutual accomplishment. The members of her group—along with their relatives—speak of her with warm devotion and remain committed to participate in her weekly sessions and community concerts. We can all thank heaven for the likes of such an angel on earth.

PONDERING

As you ponder and pray to develop and apply the divine attributes discussed in this chapter, please consider the following questions:

- In what ways can you follow the leadership examples of Esther and Deborah? How can you encourage others to do the same?

- In what ways can you better emulate the leadership of the Savior by following in His footsteps as one of His noble "saviours . . . on mount Zion" (Obadiah 1:21)?

- How is your leadership anchored in teamwork and mutual cooperation as demonstrated in Melanie's story?

- As you look around, what new opportunities present themselves to increase and augment your leadership in noble and courageous ways?

- In what ways does womanly leadership include facing and surmounting challenges of peril and danger? How can you help the sons and daughters of Zion around you to do so?

- What feelings do you have about blending your leadership patterns with love, compassion, and mercy according to the example of the Savior?

- Which individuals in your circle of friendship—both men and women—have set an example for you to embrace the opportunity to lead, guide, direct, and pilot the progress of the children of God?

- How can you more fully obtain the guidance of the Spirit in all that you do as a leader in Zion? How can this guidance assist in your reassurance that you are a child of God with a divinely appointed destiny?

CHAPTER SIX

Gifted Life

Every good gift and every perfect gift is from above, and cometh down from the Father of lights, with whom is no variableness, neither shadow of turning. (James 1:17)

THE TAPESTRY OF OUR LIVES is a blend of the threads of giving. The Lord gives us life and redemption. He is "the light and the life of the world" (D&C 12:9; D&C 39:2). He blesses us continually with mercy, grace, saving truths, hope, courage, strength, and goodness. He opens the gates of opportunity so that we, in turn, can bless others by rendering unto them our own gifts in the cause of service and compassion. As "the Father of lights" (James 1:17), He helps us light the way for others. He touches our hearts so we can touch the hearts of friends and loved ones.

These blessings are abundant in the lives of the Lord's "faithful daughters who [have] lived through the ages and worshiped the true and living God" (D&C 138:39). The eternal woman is illuminated with the glow of charity. There is warmth there. There is a love for life there. There is an understanding of our potential as children of God. The eternal woman manifests the touch of heaven, the glory of grace at work. In gratitude, we can perceive the mission of eternal womanhood as one of fostering the gifts of life and love. Perhaps we can characterize this enduring quality in poetic terms as "gifted life"—a life dedicated to giving in loving ways.

Please consider the following scenes as a gateway to greater understanding of how this eternal woman can reveal the touch of the divine in our lives and inspire us to do better each day.

1. ONE MOMENT IN ETERNITY: RACHEL
In the design of the Lord, the growth of the eternal family leads to an abundance of love. Rachel, wife of Jacob, was a memorable personality in

the unfolding of this design. Her life was one of faithful devotion to the family cause. She carried on and magnified the heavenly commission given to Sarah, wife of Abraham, to become the "mother of nations" (Genesis 17:16), and to Rebekah, the wife of Isaac, to become "the mother of thousands of millions" (Genesis 24:60). As a daughter of destiny, Rachel contributed in a central way to the unfolding of the Abrahamic covenant (see Abraham 2:8–11, also Genesis 12:2–3; 17:1–5, 20–21; 21:12–13; 22:15–18; 35:9–12). She was the mother of Joseph, through whose lineage the blessings of heaven would be extended to all quarters of the world. To her dying day, she was loyal in her calling as a wife and a mother in Zion, as the following scene reveals:

> A warm breeze caused the gentle fabric of the tent to billow in melodic rhythms. Young Joseph knelt beside his mother and held her hand tightly as she rested on the portable divan, protected by a delicate filmy canopy of white, green, and blue hangings held in place with fine linen cords. With his other hand, he gently wiped the moisture from her forehead with a soft cloth. "Are you feeling better, Mother?"
>
> Rachel responded quietly, "Yes, thank you, my son. So kind of you to ask. It was so gracious of your father to pause our journey for a time. How is he doing?"
>
> "He will return soon. He is bringing some fresh water for you from a stream flowing through the grove of trees nearby."
>
> Just then the bleating of young lambs was heard in the distance. "They are calling your name," said Joseph with a twinkle in his eyes.
>
> His mother smiled. She fondly remembered the time she had told him that the name given to her by her parents in Mesopotamia meant "ewe."
>
> She reached over and stroked his face. "You are a constant reminder of the blessings the Lord has given to our family. When we were passing through Bethel on our journey here, the Lord visited your father once again and confirmed that his new name would be Israel."[122]
>
> "What does that name mean, Mother?"
>
> "It means that he is bound to God with an eternal covenant of love and service. He is to follow in the footsteps of his father and grandfather to become 'a father of many nations.'"[123] She stroked the hair of the young lad. "When God remembered me

and blessed me with a precious son, we gave you a name that means 'increase,' for you will carry on the promise of your father to become a multitude of nations."[124]

Joseph took her hand again. "This has been a long journey, Mother. Now that we have passed through Jerusalem, we are so close to our destination of Bethlehem."

"A long journey, yes," she responded, "but also a journey of peace, a journey on which your father was able to bring harmony into our family circle once again. When the Lord commanded him to leave my homeland and take us to his kindred in the land of Canaan,[125] my father was troubled. But your father worked things out with him through the guidance of the Lord.[126] And on this journey he also reconciled the differences with his brother, Esau.[127] Your father is a man of peace—and I promise that you will also be a man of peace."

Then a faint shadow slowly settled over her face, suggesting that she was struggling with inner emotions. "Ben-oni," she whispered.[128]

"Mother, what do you mean?"

She took a deep breath. "After I had the joy of bringing you into the world, I was promised from heaven that 'The Lord shall add to me another son.'[129] That time is approaching. Ben-oni means 'son of my sorrow,' for in my pain I shall soon bring your brother into the world."[130]

At that moment a stately figure parted the folds of the doorway of the tent and entered. He came over and knelt at Rachel's side to embrace her with loving care. Gently he held a cup to her lips and poured in drops of soothing water.

She beamed a radiant smile back at him.

"You are my love," he whispered. He was fondly remembering the years he had served to earn her hand in marriage—"and they seemed unto him but a few days, for the love he had to her."[131] He thought, *I would gladly do it again and again.*

There was a moment of silence before he spoke up. "Joseph, my son. Please go and invite the midwife and the maidens to come in to her."

The hour had arrived. It would not be long before a new life would come into the world—a son to be called Benjamin by his father, meaning "son of my right hand."

But sadly, Rachel, "beautiful and well favoured,"[132] a precious daughter of destiny, a glorious example of motherhood, would pass on to a better world, leaving this mortal realm in the act of gifting life unto her son.

2. SISTERLY ECHOES: MARY, SISTER OF MARTHA

The giving of life as manifested by Rachel is a pervasive and enduring dimension of eternal womanhood. This same gift is reflected in the lives of other daughters of destiny, who sustain the power of vitality where the shadowy touch of death tries to intercede onto the scene of our hope and cheer. Mary, sister to Martha and Lazarus, was one of those. The details of her inspiring faith and compassion are given in the last part of chapter 10 of the Gospel of Luke and in chapters 11 and 12 of the Gospel of John. Perhaps the following scene can serve to confirm the welcome presence of an individual like Mary, who sustained and magnified the spirit of living hope as a devoted follower of the Master. Her gift to us is the witness that life will always triumph over death through the power of the Atonement of Jesus Christ.

The humble home in the village of Bethany, not far from Jerusalem, appeared to be languishing in darkness. Emptiness floated from corner to corner—a gloomy reminder of the absence of someone so deeply loved. Mary parted the curtain at the window and stared across the landscape toward a narrow roadway leading to the village. Far off in the distance, barely within her view, two individuals could be seen standing facing each other in the shadows of a grove of olive trees. She supposed one of the individuals to be her sister, Martha, who had left home earlier to walk to the outskirts of the village in response to the news that another visitor may be arriving soon. Visitors had been coming for the past four days to extend comfort and condolences at a time of solemn mourning for the loss of Lazarus. Who was the individual standing next to her sister in the distance?

As she squinted to gain a clearer view, she began to gather a few more sensory details of what was happening. A spark of joy flashed through her soul. The robe. The noble stature. Was this the Master? Was this the very one who had visited in their home not long ago? Was this not the one at whose feet she had knelt as she "heard his word"?[133] Was He not the one she had "anointed . . . with ointment, and wiped his feet with her hair"?[134]

Her heart was awakened with a renewed sense of hope as she recalled the glow of His face and the touch of His hand. Had he not spoken words of promise concerning her service unto Him that she "hath chosen that good part, which shall not be taken away from her"?[135]

She turned away from the window and looked about the home. It was as if a light was beginning to seep into the shadows. In her mind's eye, it seemed as though she could almost make out the image of her deceased brother smiling at her from the doorway to his room. She seemed to know now with utter clarity what she had been hoping for since his departure: that he was still alive—somehow, somewhere—and still a part of their family circle.

Her sister's words from another time echoed in her ears. Martha had said to the Master, "I know that he shall rise again in the resurrection at the last day."[136] Those words of assurance were balm to Mary's soul—but somehow, having also been close to the Master, having listened to His words and anointed His feet, she had a sense that His gift of life was more than a distant harvest; it was intended also for the here and now. The flame of hope arose more brightly within her heart. In faith and love, she whispered a quiet prayer on behalf of her departed brother.

At that moment the sound of footsteps carried her attention back to the outdoors again. Someone was moving swiftly to reach the home. Suddenly the door swung open to reveal the image of her sister Martha, panting for breath. "The Master is come, and calleth for thee."[137]

With excitement, Mary rose up without hesitation and rushed to the edge of the village to meet Him.[138] When she came to Him, weeping, "she fell down at his feet, saying unto him, Lord, if thou hadst been here, my brother had not died."[139] Looking up into His face, she saw that He too was weeping.[140]

The neighbors standing nearby, also weeping for the departed Lazarus, were heard to declare, "Behold how he loved him!"[141]

Directly, the Master went with the circle of followers to the cave where Lazarus lay entombed. When Martha expressed concern about the degeneration of the body, the Master reminded her of His words: "Said I not unto thee, that, if thou wouldest believe, thou shouldest see the glory of God?"[142] That glory was about to become manifest through a divine prayer: "And Jesus lifted up his eyes, and said, Father, I thank thee that thou hast heard me. And I knew that thou hearest me always: but because of the people which stand by I said it, that they may believe that thou hast sent me."[143]

He then called unto Lazarus, who came forth to the astonishment of all the observers. Life had been restored. Faith had been confirmed. Joy was abounding once again. What Mary had envisioned became reality. What the Master had promised her came about, for "Mary hath chosen that good part, which shall not be taken away from her."[144]

Not long afterward, at the time of Passover, Jesus returned once again to visit with the three siblings at supper time. As she had done days before, Mary knelt at the feet of her Master to serve Him as the source of all life, as the record confirms: "Then took Mary a pound of ointment of spikenard, very costly, and anointed the feet of Jesus, and wiped his feet with her hair: and the house was filled with the odour of the ointment."[145]

One of the Lord's disciples, observing the proceedings, raised the point that the costly ointment should instead have been sold to raise alms for the poor. To Judas Iscariot, the Lord replied, "Let her alone: against the day of my burying hath she kept this. For the poor always ye have with you; but me ye have not always."[146]

Mary, all along, had been embracing the faithful premonition that the Savior would soon give His life as the Lamb of God. Thus she had been serving Him with abiding love—honoring His eternal station as Redeemer. His words to the family continued to echo with power: "I am the resurrection, and the life: he that believeth in me, though he were dead, yet shall he live: And whosoever liveth and believeth in me shall never die."[147]

Mary can thus be remembered as a living example of the kind of faith and devotion that advance the cause of the Lord, and her story continues to remind us of the divine mission of the Lord to "bring to pass the immortality and eternal life of man" (Moses 1:39). Mary is an enduring sisterly echo of the lives of all the daughters of destiny who sustain and glorify the vitality of the divine plan of salvation, knowing that "the gift of God is eternal life through Jesus Christ our Lord" (Romans 6:23). In this spirit, the role of eternal womanhood continually radiates the light of life.

3. A Modern Moment: A New Life Comes into the World
All around us are caring examples of the "gifted life." As you ponder the following true account, think of the wonderful women who have blessed you and your loved ones:

> Amy was a person of heavenly gifts—enduring charity, joyful service, warm sisterhood, loving motherhood. She had a special way of looking into the shadows to find the lonely and the sad and bring them into the light of joy and togetherness. One of her friends who had worked closely
>
> **" All around us are caring examples of the 'gifted life.' "**
>
> with her in Church positions shared later these words with Amy's children: "Some people are satisfied if they are happy. Others are concerned with the happiness of friends and relatives. A few are anxious to find the stranger or lonely person and make them happy too. Your mother belonged to this last group."
>
> A mother of two, Amy was looking forward to the birth of a third gift from heaven. As with earlier pregnancies, she was having some health difficulties. For that reason, she had journeyed across the country to be treated by her brother, a celebrated obstetrician and gynecologist. But with the coming of the Christmas season, she wrote a letter to her family to share her heartfelt desires: "Christmas dinner with my family in my own home would make me very happy—just our own family, us four, no more. Maybe the cats—how about it?"
>
> Her family was thrilled, but her husband felt a sense of foreboding, as he later wrote in his journal: "I felt impressed to advise her to spend the next few months . . . under [her brother's] care."
>
> Despite these anxieties, Amy returned home to be with her family at Christmas time. In a letter to her sister on December 18th, she wrote: "I am feeling much better than I did. Oh, it seemed so good to be home again with my family. And were they glad to have me back! Yes, I surely feel that children need mothers, even though, like me, they can give only moral support. . . . Right now we are devoting all our thoughts and energies toward next May when we will have this long-awaited baby. . . . Our Christmas will be a very happy one this year because we'll be all together."

For the next few months, the family made preparations for the arrival of the new baby—the promised gift from heaven. Excitement was high. When the hour came, the children said good-bye as their parents departed for the local hospital.

One woman later shared these words with the family: "We were both at the hospital together where our babies were born. . . . That morning she had been so very sweet and kind to me by insisting that I sit down by her, and she fixed my hair very nice. She came in my room after dinner and sat, and we talked and laughed together for a long time. Then she was taken into the case room, and soon a little new life was here on earth."

Word about the baby came to her children soon thereafter, but not without shadows. One of the children later reported the experience: "During the night I recall being awakened from a deep sleep. Silhouette figures appeared in the doorway of my bedroom, illuminated from behind by the light in the hallway. A voice called out. It was the voice of my father. The news was shocking, devastating. My mother had passed away in bringing a new life into the world."

Words were inadequate to express the depth of sorrow that settled over the family in the wake of such a loss. A pall of mourning hovered over the whole community. The warmth of spring had been snuffed out. The seasons had shifted, and winter had returned. It was as if life itself was gasping for breath and for a renewal.

And yet, despite the sadness, there was a spirit of renewal that embraced all those involved—a miracle in the midst of heartbreak, an awakening in the shadows of sorrow. A new life had come into the world. A choice new baby had entered the family circle. The mother had fulfilled her mission once again as the Eve within her family, "because she was the mother of all living."[148] Looking back at this reality after decades of contemplation and pondering, her children can still see in their mother the flower of majesty, the touch of heaven, the gifted life.

PONDERING

As you contemplate your own situation and pray to develop more fully the divine attribute of the "gifted life," please consider the following questions:

- How do the examples of individuals such as Rachel, Mary (sister of Martha), and Amy help you to cultivate your own example of inspiration as one with the enduring capacity to serve with greater resolve and valor?

- In what ways can you seek and find more opportunities to follow in the footsteps of the Lord in sustaining the gift of life for all of your loved ones?

- How can you help foster increased faith and love by serving the needs of those slipping into the shadows of discouragement—especially over the loss of a loved one?

- With the blessings of the Spirit, how have you been able to find opportunities to share with others the certainty that the light of immortality will overcome the pale of temporal death? In that spirit, how can you find joy in serving as a witness that the glory of eternal life will burst forth in the due time of the Lord as an everlasting blessing for all of God's faithful sons and daughters?

- What feelings do you have in knowing that your life can also become a beacon of living joy for others, never to be extinguished?

- In what ways can you more tenderly and faithfully take to heart the Lord's promise: "And, if you keep my commandments and endure to the end you shall have eternal life, which gift is the greatest of all the gifts of God" (D&C 14:7)?

CHAPTER SEVEN

Joyful Conversion

Marvel not that all mankind, yea, men and women, all nations, kindreds, tongues and people, must be born again; yea, born of God, changed from their carnal and fallen state, to a state of righteousness, being redeemed of God, becoming his sons and daughters; And thus they become new creatures; and unless they do this, they can in nowise inherit the kingdom of God.
(Mosiah 27:25–26)

WHAT IS CONVERSION? IT IS the process of being born again—the spiritual transformation through which our sins are forgiven. We embark on the pathway toward perfection with the promise that if we endure to the end in obedience to the commandments, we will inherit eternal life. To be born again of God implies a sanctifying process by which the natural man or woman is supplanted by the new spiritual man or woman who enjoys the companionship of the Holy Ghost and hence is no longer disposed to "do evil, but to do good continually" (Mosiah 5:2). In this manner, through compliance with the principles and ordinances of the gospel, we become spiritually begotten sons and daughters of God.

The process of conversion is a divine gift of heaven that enables us to abound in joy and comfort. Conversion continues as we embrace and fulfill the callings that come to us from the Lord throughout our mortal journey. Even in perilous times, we can radiate the light of the gospel as a blessing for ourselves and those we serve.

The principle of spiritual conversion raises life-changing questions in our hearts and minds. What steps can we take to remain firmly anchored on the pathway of conversion and improve our capability to share the eternal truths of the gospel of Jesus Christ? In what ways can we help those we serve to understand how the healing and nurturing process of conversion will bring transforming blessings of joy, peace, comfort, and hope into their lives?

Answers can come to us through the word of God and the inspiration of the Holy Ghost. How does eternal womanhood contribute to this process? What examples among the daughters of Zion do we find in the scriptures to encourage us to seek the blessings of conversion continually as we strive to overcome reversals and lapses in the process of spiritual growth? How do the examples of exemplary women stimulate our own search for an enduring state of conversion? Perhaps the following scenes will help open the doors of awakening.

1. ONE MOMENT IN ETERNITY: WIFE OF KING LAMONI

The wife of King Lamoni is one of the most exemplary women depicted in the Book of Mormon. The account of her miraculous conversion, given in chapter 19 of the book of Alma, is rather brief, and she remained unnamed in the record. Nevertheless, her unshakeable faith, eulogized by her missionary teacher Ammon, remains a beacon of light for all seekers of truth. Her example of coming unto Christ with her husband was instrumental in bringing a vast flock of Lamanite people into the fold of the Lord. Perhaps the following scene will allow you to travel back in time and join with her as she goes through a miraculous process of transformation through the power of the Spirit:

> A growing sensation of hope was beginning to simmer within her soul. For two days and two nights, she had been mourning at the side of her husband, who lay silent and motionless on his bed as if he had departed from this life.
>
> But now a stately visitor from a nation to the north stood with her in the darkened room, a light of understanding and friendship radiating from his countenance. When she had summoned him, he had asked, "What would you that I should do?"[149]
>
> She had told him of her desire: "The servants of my husband have made it known unto me that thou art a prophet of a holy God, and that thou hast power to do many mighty works in his name."[150]
>
> In response to her request, the visitor looked into the eyes of the queen and confirmed the hope of her heart: "He is not dead, but he sleepeth in God, and on the morrow he shall rise again; therefore bury him not."[151]
>
> A light of relief and comfort flowed instantly into her soul as she absorbed those words. While staring down upon her beloved

husband with renewed anticipation, she thought, *One more day and he shall return to my side!* We realize that she did not yet fully savor the feelings of spiritual enlightenment burning in the heart of her visitor, Ammon—but the moment was at hand when she would be able to do so.

He knew what was about to take place, for the miracle of her husband's conversion two days previous was still burning within his memory. He had realized then "that king Lamoni was under the power of God; he knew that the dark veil of unbelief was being cast away from his mind, and the light which did light up his mind, which was the light of the glory of God, which was a marvelous light of his goodness—yea, this light had infused such joy into his soul, the cloud of darkness having been dispelled, and that the light of everlasting life was lit up in his soul, yea, he knew that this had overcome his natural frame, and he was carried away in God."[152]

Now the moment had come for the queen to have the same experience of awakening.

"He will rise again on the morrow," repeated Ammon. "Believest thou this?"[153]

She quietly answered, "I have had no witness save thy word, and the word of our servants; nevertheless I believe that it shall be according as thou hast said."[154]

He marveled at the faith and acceptance of the Lamanite queen: "Blessed art thou because of thy exceeding faith; I say unto thee, woman, there has not been such great faith among all the people of the Nephites."[155]

From that moment on until the appointed time of her husband's awakening the following day, the queen watched over the bed of her husband in joyful expectation. As prophesied, the miracle happened. A rejuvenation took place.

The king arose and stretched his hand out to his wife with words of transcendent peace: "Blessed be the name of God, and blessed art thou. For as sure as thou livest, behold, I have seen my Redeemer; and he shall come forth, and be born of a woman, and he shall redeem all mankind who believe on his name."[156]

We can observe that the queen was transfixed in her jubilation. Immediately both she and the king became overpowered by the

Spirit of God[157] and sank down into a spiritual sleep of rapture and peace.

Ammon, their visitor, dropped to his knees and poured out his prayers of thanksgiving to the Lord for the blessings of conversion flowing unto the Lamanite people.[158] Soon he too fell into a slumber of spiritual bliss, knowing that the gospel of Jesus Christ would now be accepted by countless sons and daughters of God throughout the land.

Within a short period of time, these three would again rise in majesty to launch the era of conversion among the Lamanite nation.[159] King Lamoni and his faithful wife, through their example and testimony, would become the instruments of persuasion to vast numbers of their people. The queen thus exemplifies the spiritual conversion and enduring faith that advance the cause of gospel truth in the world.

2. SISTERLY ECHOES: SARIAH

Conversion is a dynamic, lifelong process. The gateway is the miraculous passage into the fold of the Lord through baptism by water and by the Spirit. Then comes the ascent up the hill of the Lord, a process of budding and expanding conversion by embracing the cause of Zion, honoring our covenants, and fulfilling our callings with increased devotion and love. Yes, there can be mistakes that need to be corrected along the way. There might be weaknesses to be overcome and frailties to be replaced with strength and courage. But life goes on. The light of the gospel continues to inspire us. The Lord promised us: "I will go before your face. I will be on your right hand and on your left, and my Spirit shall be in your hearts, and mine angels round about you, to bear you up" (D&C 84:88).

> " Conversion is a dynamic, lifelong process. "

In this spirit of comfort, do you find familiar memories in the following living scene from the life of Sariah, wife of the prophet Lehi?

> Softly the evening sun immersed itself below the desert horizon, a purple glow undulating across the endless rolling sands. Standing near the family tent, she watched in silence, a tear descending slowly down her cheek. Another day, another sunset—more of the same agony she had been feeling ever since her sons had disappeared over the drifting dunes on their journey back toward the family home so far away.

"Home," she whispered softly, suppressing a soul-deep sigh. She pictured their abandoned but still cherished estate, filled with abundant comforts gleaned from years of careful planning and devoted effort.[160] We can hear her wistful words. "Our home is now the shifting sands in this burning wilderness. Empty and lonely and barren—just like my heart."

At that moment, a hand came gently to rest on her shoulder, causing her to lift her head and turn slowly toward the visitor. Her husband had come up from behind to intrude into her reverie of anguish. He knew of her suffering. He understood her sorrow.

"They will return," Lehi assured her. "The Lord will protect them."

Leaning herself against her husband for relief, she locked her vision on the place where the sun had just sunk from view, leaving a vacuum of emptiness on the horizon. "Just as the sun is now gone," she whispered, her voice quaking, her shoulders stooping, "they too are gone. 'My sons are no more, and we perish in the wilderness.'"[161]

He smiled gently and drew her closer. "Just as the sun will rise again on the morrow, so will our sons return, bringing with them the legacy of the word of God."

"I yearn to believe you—sincerely I do," she responded, turning to look directly into his eyes. "I should then be able to say from the depths of my heart that I know the Lord is with our sons to protect them."

Just then a mild breeze arose and gently lifted a lock of her hair upward toward her cheek as if to dry away the lonely tear suspended there. The shadows of evening continued to descend over the landscape, responding to the vanishing glow of the sun like phantom figures playfully dancing over the dunes. Entranced by the wonder of the sunset, she imagined those figures to be real. They seemed to take on the shapes of her departed sons against the now golden sky.

She hungered to see them again and know that they were safe. How she longed to hold them in her arms and weep tears of joy and relief. A strange sensation began to arise within her soul as she perceived among those distant ghostly figures the shapes and contours of a more familiar kind, like echoes of living memories floating in her mind. Though still a great distance away, it seemed to her as though they were coalescing into living beings, moving ever closer towards her.

She gasped! Could it be? Her heart soared with the sudden hope of faith. Then, above the quiet moaning of the desert breeze resounded the faint but certain voices of deliverance. "Mother! Father!"

A miracle came into view—her sons had returned in safety!

As her sons approached the family tent, voicing warm greetings, their mother exclaimed with words of unrestrained cheer the feelings of her heart: "Now I know of a surety that the Lord hath commanded my husband to flee into the wilderness; yea, and I also know of a surety that the Lord hath protected my sons, and delivered them out of the hands of Laban, and given them power whereby they could accomplish the thing which the Lord hath commanded them."[162]

In the spirit of harmony and gratitude, the family united to offer thanks unto the God of Israel. They listened to Lehi review and describe the sacred records now in their hands, conveying the rejuvenating power of the word of the prophets from the beginning of time down to their present day.[163] It was a day of awakening concerning the love of the Lord, a day of conversion to the vitality and immediacy of the plan of happiness.

Soon thereafter, the returning sons yielded to the silent beckoning of their awaiting beds and surrendered to the soothing relief of a well-earned sleep, but their mother remained awake a little longer to bask in the spirit of comfort and warmth that flowed through her being.[164] The fresh fragrance of a nearby spring of water cleansed the night air. The stars twinkled with the light of heaven. Her happiness was restored. Her soul was illuminated with love. Her hope was again reborn in the aura of conversion that is the continual companion to those who continue along the pathway of life. Her life was renewed in the Lord.

Sariah, the "goodly" mother of Nephi and his siblings (see 1 Nephi 1:1), would go forward from this moment onward to become the ancestral mother of millions of people, whose history, as recorded in the Book of Mormon, extends more than a thousand years into the future and, in fact, even to this day. Despite severe tribulation of both the global journey and the rebellion of Laman and Lemuel, Sariah would remain optimistically faithful and loyal to the commission given her by the Lord. Following Lehi's dream of the tree of life, he reported having observed his wife, along with Nephi and Sam, partaking of the fruit of the tree, "which was desirable above all other fruit" (1 Nephi 8:15). Thus Lehi provided an inspired confirmation of the righteous character of his wife and those two sons.

Few women in the flow of history have been exposed to suffering and tribulation in greater measure than Sariah. She sustained her husband in relinquishing their earthly abundance in order to obey the commandment of the Lord to flee into the desert on the eve of the destruction of Jerusalem. She spent eight years roaming in the wilderness with her family (see 1 Nephi 17:4) before journeying to a new land where the burdens of survival and the challenges of chronically rebellious sons brought wrinkles and grayness to her frame (see 1 Nephi 18:18). However, her spirit of faithful hopefulness and devotion to the Lord's cause was rekindled through the blessings of the Lord. Thus Sariah can rise among women as an exemplar of renewal and enduring conversion.

3. A MODERN MOMENT: A NAUVOO MOTHER

The fruit of living the gospel is joy—joy in the abundance of personal comfort and peace, joy in the blessings of ongoing conversion, and joy in the spiritual harvest experienced by loved ones. The following true incident reported by a faithful woman in Zion confirms this truth in a memorable way:[165]

> I was traveling with my mother and two sisters to Nauvoo, Illinois, where we were going to celebrate the majesty of the reconstructed temple and participate in endowment sessions. On our inbound flight, we made the acquaintance of another family group—also consisting of a mother and three daughters—en route to the same destination. They were friendly and sociable people, the kind one enjoys getting to know. During our visit to some of the historical sites in the "City of Joseph," we were pleased to encounter our new friends once again. They were exuberant and joyful—with a special light in their eyes.
>
> As their mother smiled, one of the daughters explained the life-changing experience of the occasion. They had traveled with their mother to visit Nauvoo, thinking that only the daughters would be entering the sacred precincts of the house of the Lord to attend an endowment session. They were anticipating that their

mother would be waiting for them to finish their temple session before continuing with their tour.

When the daughters were preparing to go over to the temple, they were amazed to hear their mother say, "I am going with you." They were overjoyed to learn that she now had a temple recommend and had already attended the temple in her home area. She had waited until Nauvoo to surprise them with the news. With rejoicing and thanksgiving, the little group of mother and daughters entered the temple to savor the blessings of that holy place—together.

"Let the heavens rejoice, and let the earth be glad" intoned the Psalmist.[166] How dear was this moment in time when the mother gave a beautiful gift to her daughters, for she had walked the pathway of the Savior and had become more like Him through her faith and prayers and spiritual awakening. She had understood the doctrine expressed by the Savior in His magnificent intercessory prayer: "And for their sakes I sanctify myself, that they also might be sanctified through the truth."[167] Truly this mother, by sanctifying herself, had sanctified her daughters as well, for she loved them as her most precious possessions and wanted more than anything to preserve the sanctity of their eternal family. Her act of faith confirmed the power of the words of the Lord: "But learn that he who doeth the works of righteousness shall receive his reward, even peace in this world, and eternal life in the world to come."[168]

Through their example, the daughters had contributed to the spiritual growth of their mother; through her example, the mother had bestowed a great blessing of joy on her daughters. They rejoiced together, understanding the precious message of Ruth: "For whither thou goest, I will go; and where thou lodgest, I will lodge: thy people shall be my people, and thy God my God."[169] They had experienced together the miracle of conversion.

There is no greater joy than that of becoming more and more like the Savior. That is the power of conversion. Let us therefore strive to bring this higher joy into our own lives as well as into the lives of others through covenant obedience and "the pure love of Christ" (Moroni 7:47). That is "becoming" in the most authentic sense. That is ongoing conversion, as Joseph Smith explained:

We consider that God has created man with a mind capable of instruction, and a faculty which may be enlarged in proportion to the heed and diligence given to the light communicated from heaven to the intellect; and that the nearer man approaches perfection, the clearer are his views, and the greater his enjoyments, till he has overcome the evils of his life and lost every desire for sin; and like the ancients, arrives at that point of faith where he is wrapped in the power and glory of his Maker and is caught up to dwell with Him. But we consider that this is a station to which no man ever arrived in a moment: he must have been instructed in the government and laws of that kingdom by proper degrees, until his mind is capable in some measure of comprehending the propriety, justice, equality, and consistency of the same. (*Teachings of the Prophet Joseph Smith*, sel. Joseph Fielding Smith [Salt Lake City: Deseret Book, 1976], p. 51.)

PONDERING

As you ponder and pray to make the process of conversion an ongoing blessing in your own life and the lives of your loved ones, please consider the following questions:

- Do the stories of the wife of King Lamoni, Sariah, and the Nauvoo mother kindle ideas and thoughts in your mind about how to rise above tribulation and achieve greater joy through a higher level of spiritual renewal?

- In your own experience, how does the Spirit of the Lord inspire you from time to time, causing your destiny as a child of God to be unfolded more fully?

- In what ways can you share with others the opportunity to become spiritually reborn and thus enjoy the blessings of conversion?

- How can the following promise of the Lord empower your life and the lives of your loved ones? "But learn that he who doeth the works of righteousness shall receive his reward, even peace in this world and eternal life in the world to come" (D&C 59:23).

- What thoughts come to your mind as you consider the role of love in the conversion process?

- What are your feelings as you consider the example of others around you or in your family history who have overcome adversity and thus savored the peace and tranquility of the gospel?

- What does it mean to "sanctify" yourself (John 17:19)? How can you help sanctify others?

- How can you express more fully your gratitude to Heavenly Father and His Son for the blessings of spiritual rebirth and conversion?

CHAPTER EIGHT

Attuned Allegiance

*He created man, male and female, after his own image and
in his own likeness, created he them; And gave unto them
commandments that they should love and serve him, the only
living and true God, and that he should be the only being
whom they should worship.* (D&C 20:18–19)

ALLEGIANCE IS A NOBLE QUALITY that defines faithful and enduring loyalty
and service. When we love and serve God, we also love and serve His
prophets, our "fellowcitizens with the saints" (Ephesians 2:19), and those
within our family circle. The greatest manifestation of allegiance is the
relationship of the Son with the Father: "But, behold, my Beloved Son,
which was my Beloved and Chosen from the beginning, said unto me—
Father, thy will be done, and the glory be thine forever" (Moses 4:2). In that
same spirit, the sons and daughters of God can cultivate allegiance to the
Savior through the blessings of the Spirit: "Wherefore, ye must press forward
with a steadfastness
in Christ, having a
perfect brightness of
hope, and a love of
God and of all men.
Wherefore, if ye shall

> **"The greatest manifestation of
> allegiance is the relationship of
> the Son with the Father."**

press forward, feasting upon the word of Christ, and endure to the end,
behold, thus saith the Father: Ye shall have eternal life" (2 Nephi 31:20).

The role of eternal womanhood aspires to the quality of attuned
allegiance, the kind of loyalty founded upon a harmonious personal
relationship with our Savior and Redeemer. Great and buoyant examples
of that kind of attuned allegiance are preserved in the scriptures.

1. ONE MOMENT IN ETERNITY: MARY MAGDALENE

Can you image the transcendent power of the experiences of a faithful young woman, Mary Magdalene, a tender follower of Jesus during His earthly ministry? Some details of these happenings are given throughout the Gospels of the New Testament, especially in Matthew 27, Mark 16, Luke 24, and John 20. Let us go back to these events as silent observers of the miracle that transpired.

> She stood outside the sepulchre in a daze of loneliness. The emptiness of the tomb, acting as a ponderous weight upon her being, left her contending with swirling emotions of both love and agony—love for her divine Master and agony over His absence. Her memories, like shadowy visitors from the past, were flowing back into her mind.
>
> She remembered with fondness how her Master had earlier blessed her and many other women in Galilee and cured them of their infirmities.[170] Perhaps she recalled how they had cheerfully shared with Him of their substance as He taught them of His mission of redemption and love.[171] But where was He now?
>
> She had been among the group of women who had followed after Him with loyalty on His final journey into Jerusalem, ministering to Him in the spirit of caring and service.[172] But where was He now?
>
> She had also been present on Golgotha, hovering at His feet along with His mother as He hung on the cross in His dying hour.[173] And she had been there with the grieving women who came and observed the sepulchre where His body was laid to rest,[174] afterward preparing aromatic spices and ointments to take to Him.[175] But where was He now?
>
> She thought of that morning in the recent past when she had been searching for her Lord and was startled to encounter an angel in the empty tomb. With feelings of both agony and love over the missing body, she had run obediently to inform the disciples of the developing situation.[176] She vividly recalled returning with Peter and John to the empty tomb, only to remain outside, weeping—not yet comprehending the impending good news of the resurrection.[177]
>
> The image of the two angels who appeared in the tomb after the Apostles had departed was coming alive in her mind once again.[178]

Did they not comfort her with a kind and glorious promise? The flickering of hope was now still present in her heart. But nevertheless, she remained inconsolable and perceived only the emptiness of the tomb. Where was her Master? Somehow the heartening angelic words spoken earlier remained, almost unperceived and unheard as a distant echo in her mind: "He is risen."[179]

It was in this crucial moment that she was caught up in an all-consuming vibrancy of conflicts within her being: the glow of enduring affection for her dearest Friend, in contrast with the darkness of her intense mourning; the flame of unshakeable loyalty to the sublime Master, in contrast with the bleakness of anxiety over His loss; the glory of her everlasting allegiance to the eternal King, in contrast with the midnight of fear that the separation was permanent. This wrenching blend of feelings within her soul aroused an overpowering need for healing answers.

She knelt down on the earth, head bowed, hands clasped together. When was there to be relief? What would be the resolution? What was the meaning of the consoling words "He is risen" that started now to re-emerge into her consciousness? Where was her Messiah?

Then she heard the snap of a twig. Startled, she looked up in the direction of the sound. Through her moistened eyes, she made out a shadowy figure beginning to appear in the distance. Was it the gardener? Could he perhaps show her the location of the vanished body? She rose to her feet.

With a tingling of expectation, she focused her attention on this stranger. He came closer and closer. "Woman, why weepest thou?" he asked. "Whom seekest thou?"[180]

When she responded that she was seeking Her Master, He said one word that engendered within her the power of recognition, one word that ignited within her soul a blaze of ecstasy and delight.

"Mary."[181] In that instant, she knew that she was facing the living Christ, the resurrected Lord, the returning Master! In joy and rapture, she became in that moment a renewed person, a person transformed by the power of grace, the first witness of this transcendent miracle in all the world.

Mary Magdalene is an enduring example of allegiance to the Lord. James E. Talmage captures the essence of her role in the earthly ministry of Jesus: "Mary Magdalene became one of the closest friends Christ had among women; her devotion to Him as her Healer and as the One whom she adored as the Christ was unswerving; she stood close by the cross while other women tarried afar off in the time of His mortal agony; she was among the first at the sepulchre on the resurrection morning, and was the first mortal to look upon and recognize a resurrected Being—the Lord whom she had loved with all the fervor of spiritual adoration" (James E. Talmage, *Jesus the Christ* [Salt Lake City, 1981], p. 264).

As the first witness of the resurrected Lord, Mary Magdalene went down in history as the exemplar of one who bears testimony of the divinity of our Lord with authenticity and enduring devotion, being attuned to the Savior with all of her heart, might, mind, and soul. In this way, she manifests in her attuned allegiance, one of the dearest qualities of eternal womanhood.

2. SISTERLY ECHOES: ABISH

The allegiance of Mary Magdalene is a key ingredient of eternal womanhood as reflected in the lives of other womanly figures honored in the pages of sacred writ. One of these figures is Abish, a Lamanite woman whose loyalty to the Lord was manifested in her decisive action to restore harmony at a time of serious contention in her community. Only a few details are known concerning Abish (see chapter 19 of the book of Alma)—but her example can inspire all the sons and daughters of God who find themselves in situations requiring courage in support of gospel principles.

> Tears pooled in her eyes as she observed with anguish the growing spirit of contention festering among the people assembled in the house of King Lamoni. Some observers were pointing toward the bodies—the queen, her husband, and their collapsed servants lying prostrate on the floor. She could hear them murmuring that a spirit of evil had destroyed the royal couple because of the visiting Nephite, also stretched out lifeless on the floor before them.[182] Others insisted that the king's fate stemmed from his actions in slaying his servants when they could not save his flocks from invaders.[183] The uproar continued to expand in volume and intensity.
>
> "What have I done in calling the people here?" whispered the woman. "It is the power of God that caused my mistress and her husband to collapse in a state of joy and rapture as they learned

divine truth!" She looked anxiously around the room. "Why are they acting so?" she asked herself. "Did I not run from house to house to gather the people here so that they would see what happened and believe in the power of God?"[184]

At that moment, a brutish figure raced toward the body of the Nephite, lifting a sword into the air with a haughty announcement. "You will die for having slain my brother while he contended for the flocks of the king!" But while brandishing his sword, he suddenly collapsed lifeless to the earth.[185]

The people recoiled in horror, some of them exclaiming that the Nephite visitor had been sent by the Great Spirit, while others contended that he was but a monster sent to torment them.[186]

Abish, the faithful servant of the queen, began to sink into the darkness of despair—rescued only by a refreshing and soothing memory that she had been guarding in secret for many years. It was a reminiscence of her father sharing with her a remarkable vision granted unto him that brought about her own conversion to the Lord.[187] She had been yearning for years to share her witness with the people—and now the events in the house of the king had opened a doorway to show forth the power of God. Breathing a deep and empowering breath, she said to herself, "I love the Lord. I cannot fail in my loyalty to Him now."

She then stepped forward from the shadows as the crowd watched in amazement. Boldly she strode over to the collapsed queen, took her by the hand, and caused her to rise and stand and shout with a loud voice: "O blessed Jesus, who has saved me from an awful hell! O blessed God, have mercy on this people!"[188]

The miracle then continued. The queen took the king by the hand and caused him to arise. He proclaimed with power a profound message to soothe and pacify the people, sharing the truths taught by Ammon. All who listened receptively to his voice were converted.[189] The Nephite visitor and the servants of the king also regained their strength and confirmed the message of truth being sent forth among the people.

Abish, the courageous woman who raised the queen, was filled with ecstasy to observe many of her Lamanite brothers and sisters responding with grateful hearts to the Spirit poured out in the royal household. Her allegiance to the Lord was magnified that day by the power of conversion. Like Ammon and the royal couple, Abish had also manifested her witness that being attuned to the Lord of Hosts in faithful allegiance is the key to eternal progression and everlasting joy.

Thus we can view Abish as a worthy instrument in the hands of the Lord, having contributed her part in the miraculous events leading to the commencement of the work of the Lord among the Lamanites: "Thus the Lord did begin to pour out his Spirit upon them; and we see that his arm is extended to all people who will repent and believe on his name" (Alma 19:36). Abish is therefore a sisterly echo of the loyalty of Mary Magdalene over a century later and a further model of how such attuned allegiance to the Lord and obedience to His gospel plan can be applied today in the lives of all the faithful sons and daughter of God.

3. A MODERN MOMENT: LOYALTY ON THE PLAINS

What we are calling "attuned allegiance" is an eternal principle that unfolds in the lives of many noble women—even on the prairies of the pioneer exodus to the Salt Lake Valley. Read the details of this modern event and ask yourself what thoughts and feelings arise in your heart.

Nighttime began to settle over the campground.[190] The noise of invisible crickets added variety to the whispering melodies of the westerly breezes. Plumes of smoke were rising from a dozen fires still smoldering in the shadows. The cries of several infants could be heard from time to time amidst the lowing of cattle.

Catharine, wife of Orson Spencer, lay silently beneath a blanket stretched over a straw bed in the covered wagon. Her breathing was punctuated at times by raspy coughs, a sign of her desperate illness. Kneeling beside her was her husband, holding her hand in tenderness. It was the eighteenth day of their journey from Nauvoo toward their new home in the West. Unending persecution had forced them to abandon their home and honor a prophet's directive to go wherever the Lord would have them go.

Dreams of a better world strengthened their hope and reinforced their faith. Catharine looked around at the circle of their children sleeping nearby within the wagon.

"My love, may I bring you some water?" her husband asked.

"I'm fine," she responded faintly with a smile. "What was the disturbance in the camp that I heard earlier?"

"It was Porter Rockwell arriving with some mail from the East."

"Something for us?" She wanted to know.

"Yes, my dear. There was a letter from your parents."

She sighed. Across her mind flowed the melancholy memory of the day in western Massachusetts when her parents had demanded that she abandon her commitment to the so-called Mormon Church, threatening to disown her if she did not recant. But her allegiance to the restored gospel of Jesus Christ was fixed and firm, and she was baptized into the faith—even at the cost of being renounced by her parents.

"What do they write?" she asked her husband.

"You remember that I wrote to them a letter from Nauvoo, pleading with them to permit you to return to them, at least until we could find a place where we could rest in security."

"Yes, I remember."

He held her hands more firmly and leaned over into the candlelight. "Well, in their response they say they would welcome you back . . ." She raised her head and opened her eyes in surprise.

Then he continued their words: ". . . but never as a member of the Mormon Church." He lowered the letter and watched in sadness as his wife lowered her head once again and turned aside in silence.

With tears trickling down his cheeks, he pled with her on bended knees to return to her parents under any circumstances until her health could be restored.

She looked up at him with a faint smile and said softly, "Orson, the Bible is there in the corner of the wagon; will you hand it to me?" He picked up the Bible and brought it over to his wife. She continued, "Now turn to the first chapter of the book of Ruth and read the fifteenth and sixteenth verses."

He knew precisely what was stated there but read the words aloud softly to fulfill her request: "Entreat me not to leave thee, or to return from following after thee. For whither thou goest, I will go; and thy people shall be my people and thy God, my God."

His voice broke, and he could read no more. His heart was overcome by the strength and devotion of his dear wife. He laid the Bible back in its place and turned to Catharine. He saw a peaceful look move across her countenance. He saw her eyelids droop and then close, signaling her silent passage to a higher world.

The following morning, there by the side of the lonely prairie road, they laid to rest this wonderful woman, Catharine Curtis Spencer. Within an hour, the caravan was again on its way. Orson Spencer sat on the driver's bench of the covered wagon, his five little children close to him, moving westward to their destiny—alone but not alone, for the Lord was with them and the memory of a sweet wife and mother remained forever.

The oldest child took the place of the mother in helping to raise the family. And when that little girl grew up, Aurelia Spencer Rogers honored the spirit of allegiance and love of her mother and became, in the year 1878, the founder of the Primary Association of the Church.[191]

The example of attuned allegiance displayed in the life of Catharine Spencer is a stirring confirmation of the strength of character that flows from enduring devotion to the Lord and His divine plan for the salvation and exaltation of the families of Zion.

PONDERING

As you think about the stories of individuals like Mary Magdalene, Abish, and Catharine Spencer, perhaps your mind gathers ideas and plans concerning your own attuned allegiance to the Lord and how you can strengthen your loyalty to Him. Consider the following questions and others that might come to your mind:

- How does your allegiance to the Lord inspire and motivate your allegiance and service to your family members and friends?

- In turn, how does your allegiance to your family members and friends inspire and motivate your allegiance and service to the Lord? Is that not a rising spiral of blessings?

- What are your feelings about the power of spiritual allegiance to bring more harmony, peace, and joy into the lives of all the sons and daughters of the Lord?

- In what ways does the loyalty of Mary Magdalene inspire you to be a faithful witness of the mission and love of the Savior? In what ways can you bless the lives of others by sharing that testimony of the divinity of the Lord and His atoning sacrifice?

- Which noble and faithful women in your life and family lineage have set an example of attuned allegiance—harmonious loyalty—to the Lord and His Church?

- How can you become more attuned to the Lord, more related to Him in the spirit of peace, harmony, and devotion?

- How does your allegiance to the Lord and His leaders enable you to willingly make your covenant sacrifice of a broken heart and a contrite spirit as you move forward toward the blessings of eternal life?

CHAPTER NINE

Heavenly Peace

Be perfect, be of good comfort, be of one mind, live in
peace; and the God of love and peace shall be with you.
(2 Corinthians 13:11)

PEACE, ONE OF THE MOST desired and cherished of conditions, is a divine endowment of love and mercy from the Almighty. Peace flows into our lives when we follow the gospel path in righteousness and with enduring commitment and faith. The paragon of peace is our Redeemer, Jesus Christ. He was introduced into the world by a choir of angels singing an anthem of peace: "Glory to God in the highest, and on earth peace, good will toward men" (Luke 2:14). He departed from this world leaving an endowment of peace for His followers: "Peace I leave with you, my peace I give unto you: not as the world giveth, give I unto you. Let not your heart be troubled, neither let it be afraid" (John 14:27).

> " Peace flows into our lives when we follow the gospel path in righteousness and with enduring commitment and faith. "

He renewed His promise of peace in the days of the Restoration: "Learn of me, and listen to my words; walk in the meekness of my Spirit, and you shall have peace in me. I am Jesus Christ; I came by the will of the Father, and I do his will" (D&C 19:23–24). And He extended the blessings of peace to reach from this mortal experience into the eternities: "But learn that he who doeth the works of righteousness shall receive his reward, even peace in this world, and eternal life in the world to come" (D&C 59:23).

The qualities of eternal womanhood include comforting peace flowing from acts of charity and kindness. A week after founding the Relief Society in Nauvoo on March 17, 1842, Joseph Smith remarked, as noted previously (see chapter 2), that the women involved included "some of our most intelligent, humane, philanthropic and respectable ladies; and we are well assured from a knowledge of those pure principles of benevolence that flow spontaneously from their humane and philanthropic bosoms, that with the resources they will have at command, they will fly to the relief of the stranger; they will pour in oil and wine to the wounded heart of the distressed; they will dry up the tears of the orphan and make the widow's heart to rejoice" (*HC* 4:567).

In the garden of mortality, the honorable daughters of Zion plant seeds of peace, nurture relationships of harmony, and help harvest the fruit of mutual accord. Said the Lord in our day: "And above all things, clothe yourselves with the bond of charity, as with a mantle, which is the bond of perfectness and peace" (D&C 88:125). Despite the myriad trials in this life, so many of the daughters of God are adorned with a mantle of heavenly peace! Through courage in transcending tribulations, so many of the mothers in Zion earn the love and admiration of their children and all others who depend upon them!

1. ONE MOMENT IN ETERNITY: EMMA SMITH

For all sons and daughters of the Lord, perfection is an eternal goal. We all long for the everlasting peace awaiting us in the mansions of heaven. Is our preparation of a perfect nature in this world? In the King Follett Sermon given by the Prophet Joseph Smith on April 7, 1844, he gave us an important insight concerning this question:

> When you climb up a ladder, you must begin at the bottom, and ascend step by step, until you arrive at the top; and so it is with the principles of the gospel—you must begin with the first, and go on until you learn all the principles of exaltation. But it will be a great while after you have passed through the veil before you will have learned them. It is not all to be comprehended in this world; it will be a great work to learn our salvation and exaltation even beyond the grave. (*Discourses of the Prophet Joseph Smith*, ed. Alma P. Burton [Salt Lake City: Deseret Book, 1977], p. 342)

We strive in this world to overcome our mortal weaknesses and move up the ladder of salvation through the process of repentance. As Nephi stated, "For we know that it is by grace that we are saved, after all we can do" (2 Nephi 25:23). We do all we can through the help of the Lord. We're not yet perfect, but it is through the miracle of faithful rejuvenation that we can progress forward as Moroni confirmed: "Then is his grace sufficient for you, that by his grace ye may be perfect in Christ" (Moroni 10:32).

The qualities of eternal womanhood serve as sentinels on the road to perfection, toward that eternal peace for which we yearn. Are the women of Zion to be considered perfect? No, since only the Father and the Son are perfect. Nevertheless the women in our lives are perfect *reminders* as daughters of God that we can all do better in our covenant obedience. In his October 2013 General Conference talk, "The Moral Force of Women," Elder Todd Christofferson expressed his commitment to avoid overpraising the women of the Church in ways that might make them feel uncomfortable. At the same time, he felt impressed to confirm that their moral authority is fundamentally vital to the building up of Zion—no matter what their station in life might be (see *Ensign*, November 2013).

Without overpraising, we thank the Lord for the example of our mothers and daughters, our sisters and aunts, the cherished women in our ancestry line, and all the faithful daughters of Eve "who [have] lived through the ages and worshiped the true and living God" (D&C 138:39). Each of these individuals can provide a lasting influence, in spite of her individual weaknesses or varying circumstances. Each can encourage the continuing process of attaining heavenly peace.

One example of such a woman was Emma Smith, wife of the Prophet Joseph. There are few women of Zion who were more greatly tested than Emma. The rancor of misjudgment and abuse that continually descended upon her husband extended also to his wife and his children. However, her devotion to the cause of the Lord was an anchor in her life, and despite her weaknesses, she manifested admirable dedication to her husband. Even his martyrdom did not cause her faith to fail. As such, Emma, first president of the Relief Society Organization of the Church, can rise as a choice exemplar of true devotion in the quest of eternal peace.

Would you please consider the following scene from among her many experiences and see what thoughts and feelings might come to you on how you might find more peace in this world as you aspire to merit the eternal peace in the world to come?

She was sitting quietly in the shadows toward the back of the assembly room, holding the tiny twins in a warm embrace, keeping them nestled in the comfort of a soft blanket. How she must have missed her own twins, who had lived but a few hours after birth just a year earlier. Now these adopted twins were also struggling with illness.

The previous night had been catastrophic. Mobsters had invaded the area and attacked her husband with unrestrained cruelty, leaving one of the twins perilously exposed to the frosty elements.[192]

Emma looked around at the group assembled for Sunday worship. An eerie sensation was invading her consciousness. Could some of those present have been part of the enemy mob during the night?

Her husband stood erect at the head of the room, presenting his Sabbath sermon. His face was scarred and bandaged. How she had mourned throughout the night over his excruciating pains and suffering. She had worked for hours with others at the Father Johnson estate to peel from her husband's scorched skin the steaming tar and ceremonial feathers of cruelty that had been applied amidst scornful laughter by the mob.

He had been bruised and beaten mercilessly—but his voice on this Sabbath morning was resolute and uplifting. She listened to his sermon—about the gospel of Jesus Christ and the principles of faith and forgiveness. She looked into the faces of those in attendance and saw tears of understanding running down many cheeks. The deep breathing of solace and admiration echoed throughout the room.

How she admired her husband. Her devotion to him was second only to her devotion to the Lord. The words of the revelation received on her behalf less than two years previous flowed again into her mind: "Behold, thy sins are forgiven thee, and thou art an elect lady, whom I have called. . . . And the office of thy calling shall be for a comfort unto my servant, Joseph Smith, Jun., thy husband, in his afflictions, with consoling words, in the spirit of meekness."[193]

She had been faithfully supporting him in his ministry. She was serving with compassion as a mother to their children. She was laboring on a divinely commissioned anthology of spiritual hymns.[194] She knew of her husband's greatness and valor before the Lord. She knew that unimaginable sacrifice and overwhelming burdens still lay ahead, but she was prepared, for the cause of Zion would proceed forth according to the design of heaven.

As her husband completed his words of inspiration that day, she felt the whisperings of the Spirit informing her that some of the visitors in the room would soon seek baptism as a result of the spiritual outpouring.[195]

She smiled a smile of consolation while embracing with motherly love and dedication the tiny twins still asleep on her lap.

Sadly, young Joseph S. Murdock, one of the adopted twins, who had contracted a severe illness during the mob attack, passed away four days later, just one day shy of eleven months of age.[196]

But the work of the Restoration continued unabated. In the wake of upheaval flows the grace of consolation; through the shadows of oppression beams the light of peace.

Mothers such as Emma are devoted nurturers who intimately know the depth of love that binds families together. When loved ones are absent, the anguish can be consuming; when loved ones perish, the longing for heavenly comfort exceeds all measure. But hope is enlisted, and faith is arrayed. What is eternally bonded will prevail.

On October 13, 1832, just over six months after the stressful tar-and-feathering scene, Joseph wrote to Emma while he was fulfilling a Church project in New York. His words confirm his love for his wife and his admiration for her character and devotion:

> I returned to my room to meditate and calm my mind and behold the thoughts of home of Emma and Julia [their surviving adopted child] rush upon my mind like a flood, and I could wish for a moment to be with them. My breast is filled with all the feelings and tenderness of a parent and a husband, and could I be with you, I would tell you many things. . . . I hope you will excuse me for writing this letter so soon after writing, for I feel as if I wanted to . . . say something to you to comfort you in your peculiar trial and present affliction. [She was at the time expecting their fourth child.] I hope God will give you strength that you may not faint. I pray God to soften the hearts of those around you to be kind to you and take . . . [the] burden off your shoulders as much as possible and not afflict you. I feel for you, for I know your state and that others do not, but you must comfort yourself knowing that God is your friend in heaven and that you have

one true and living friend on earth, your husband. (*The Personal Writings of Joseph Smith*, compiled and edited by Dean C. Jessee [Salt Lake City: Deseret Book, 1984], p. 253; spelling and punctuation updated)

During Joseph's imprisonment in Liberty Jail, Emma wrote to him on March 7, 1839, to express her feelings of anguish on his behalf and on behalf of all the suffering Saints:

> I shall not attempt to write my feelings altogether, for the situation in which you are, the walls, bars, and bolts, rolling rivers, running streams, rising hills, sinking valleys, and spreading prairies that separate us, and the cruel injustice that first cast you into prison and still holds you there, with many other considerations, places my feelings far beyond description. Was it not for conscious innocence, and the direct interposition of divine mercy, I am very sure I never should have been able to have endured the scenes of suffering that I have passed through, since what is called the Militia, came into Far West, under the ever-to-be remembered Governor's notable order [extermination of the Mormons]. . . . We are all well at present, except Frederick, who is quite sick. Little Alexander, who is now in my arms, is one of the finest little fellows you ever saw in your life. He is so strong that with the assistance of a chair he will run all round the room. . . .
>
> No one but God, knows the reflections of my mind and the feelings of my heart when I left our house and home and almost all of everything that we possessed excepting our little children, and took my journey out of the State of Missouri, leaving you shut up in that lonesome prison. But the recollection is more than human nature ought to bear. . . .
>
> The daily sufferings of our brethren in travelling and camping out nights, and those on the other side of the river would beggar the most lively description. The people in this state are very kind indeed; they are doing much more than we ever anticipated they would. I have many more things I could like to write but have not time and you may be astonished at my bad writing and incoherent manner, but you will pardon all when you reflect how hard it would be for you to write, when your hands were stiffened with hard work and your heart convulsed with intense anxiety. But I hope there [are] better days to come to us yet. (*The Personal*

Writings of Joseph Smith, compiled and edited by Dean C. Jessee [Salt Lake City: Deseret Book, 1984], p. 388–389; spelling and punctuation updated)

From such writings we are reminded that it is the Lord who calls us on our journey. He sends us on our quest. In His strength we can overcome life's challenges. Separation is but a moment. Reunion will come as surely as the sun will rise again. We are grateful for the design of heaven bringing us together. We are thankful for the plan of happiness opening up the vista of everlasting comfort in the presence of those we love. Though we face continual tribulation—whether inward or external—there is a blessing awaiting the patient, the faithful, and the devoted. It is a blessing of peace and glory bestowed by a merciful Lord as certain as the rising sun. For this we offer unto the Lord our devotion in the spirit of quiet thanksgiving— and we rejoice in the constant renewal of our faith.

The women of Zion, like Emma Smith and countless other faithful sisters, know in their hearts that the Lord loves them and reaches out to them in compassion and mercy—especially during days of tribulation and trial. As the Psalmist declared: "The Lord will give strength unto his people; the Lord will bless his people with peace" (Psalm 29:11). And Paul declared, "For God is not the author of confusion, but of peace" (1 Corinthians 14:33). In the same spirit, eternal womanhood sustains the pattern of bringing peace and harmony into the lives of God's children, for that is the design of a loving Father and His Only Begotten Son.

2. SISTERLY ECHOES: LUCY MACK SMITH

The devotion of Emma Smith as an advocate of peace demonstrates a key dimension of eternal womanhood. That same quality also radiated from the life of the mother of the Prophet Joseph, Lucy Mack Smith, who displayed throughout her days a commitment to follow the counsel of the Lord "that ye should live in peace one with another" (Mosiah 2:20). Consider the following scene and examine your feelings about love and honor and devotion:

It was Wednesday, October 8, 1845. The revered and aging mother of the martyred Prophet Joseph stood noble and firm, looking out across the vast assembly of some five thousand Saints. Brigham Young had invited her to speak words of counsel to the sons and daughters of the Church. It was a moment where hearts yearned for hope and souls longed for peace. It was the last conference of the Church to be held in Nauvoo and the first associated with the nearly completed temple.[197]

In the spirit of motherhood, Lucy Mack Smith exhorted all to protect their children from idleness by giving them work to do and books to read. She gave words of cheerful counsel: "Be full of love, goodness and kindness, and never to do in secret, what you would not do in the presence of millions."[198]

Then in a gracious gesture, she asked the congregation, "Might you consider me to be a mother in Israel?"[199]

To this request, Brigham Young responded with the proposal, "All who consider Mother Smith as a mother in Israel, signify it by saying yes!"

The crowd then rang out with one universal "Yes!"[200]

Receiving this unanimous salutation with gratitude, she then recounted with deep emotion the travails of her family and the sacrifice of her son Joseph as the Prophet of the Restoration. Referring to the occasion when Missouri authorities had threatened him with summary execution, she recalled pressing through the crowd to be with him and savor his words of comfort: "God bless you, my dear Mother!"[201]

> " Through compassion and love, the daughters of Zion radiate the truth and beauty of the gospel. "

Thoughts of comfort and peace streamed through her mind. As she stood in silence for a moment before the admiring assembly, she remembered Joseph sharing with her the vision of the celestial kingdom he had received in the Kirtland Temple nearly a decade earlier: "I saw Father Adam and Abraham; and my father and my mother; my brother Alvin, that has long since slept."[202] She enjoyed the comfort of that inspired vision.

When her remarks were finished, she returned to her chair and peered off toward the western horizon, knowing with certainty that the Saints would soon find a new home in the West, where a greater measure of peace would come as a blessing from the Lord.

Like her daughter-in-law Emma, Lucy was nurtured by the gospel of peace. The Lord—"The Prince of Peace" (Isaiah 9:6)—promised,

"Blessed are the peacemakers: for they shall be called the children of God" (Matthew 5:9; see also 3 Nephi 12:9). To His disciples He said, "Peace be unto you" (Luke 24:36; John 20:19, 21, 26). Paul said, "And be at peace among yourselves" (1 Thessalonians 5:13).

Eternal womanhood ensures the essence of peace in the family of God. Through compassion and love, the daughters of Zion radiate the truth and beauty of the gospel. The scriptures confirm the nobility and honor of all who publish peace: "And O how beautiful upon the mountains were their feet! And again, how beautiful upon the mountains are the feet of those that are still publishing peace! And again, how beautiful upon the mountains are the feet of those who shall hereafter publish peace, yea, from this time henceforth and forever!" (Mosiah 15:15–17).

"To be spiritually minded is life and peace," declared Paul (Romans 8:6). The message of the women of Zion who reflect this characteristic endures forever: "And let the peace of God rule in your hearts, to the which also ye are called in one body; and be ye thankful" (Colossians 3:15).

3. A Modern Moment: The Memory Photograph[203]

The following true account by a priesthood leader confirms the blessings of peace that flow from the love of motherhood:

A spirit of peace and contentment hovered over the elderly residents of the nursing home during the sacrament service. That morning they sang or hummed to the melodies of the hymns with nods and smiles, savoring the words and music as if streams of strength were flowing into their lives of frailty and infirmity.

My heart was filled with gratitude as I observed the devoted service of the young people in our ward who had come that day in the capacity of shepherds of love to serve and encourage, teach and inspire, lift and hearten. My eyes scanned the room to look into the faces of the several dozen residents present. There was a glow about them, a sense of rediscovering the energy of youth that once had filled their lives.

For some reason, my attention came to focus on a woman sitting alone at the back of the room, clutching in her hand a small object. She appeared fragile and gaunt but still alert and eager to participate with her friends in the spirit of Sunday worship.

After the service came to an end, I followed my impression to walk over and visit with her. I greeted her and sat down next to her to wait for her response. She smiled and reached the object up for me to see.

Although unable to communicate in words, she spoke with her eyes and her smile. It was a small black-and-white photograph. She pointed to a little girl in the picture, standing next to a pleasant-looking woman with her arms around the girl in a gesture of motherly tenderness. Then she pointed to herself.

Clearly the photograph was a snapshot from her youth, a reminder of a tender time with her mother. Now the picture, like her frame, was bent; and like her countenance, the image was wrinkled. But there was little doubt that fond memories were at work in her heart—memories of love that would keep the flame of life alive until the Lord in His wisdom should deem the battle over, the mission complete.

Thoughts flowed into my mind as I joined silently with her on this special occasion. In the wrinkles and folds of adversity are hidden the seeds of faith. In the often lonely struggles of life are found the nurturing seedbeds where hope can sprout anew again and again, and the spirit can rise in majesty as "a tree springing up unto everlasting life."[204]

The Spirit whispered to me the certainty of the situation. Someday soon this tender lady would return to the spirit world where vast congregations of the Lord's children await the coming resurrection and a return to the realms of glory.[205] She would then embrace her loving mother, rejoicing in memories past, and together they would look forward to attaining the heavenly gift of eternal peace and ever-burning light.

What was preserved in that wrinkled picture would then become a living reality. What was sealed in her aging heart would blossom as the timeless fruit of the eternal family.

Pondering

As you ponder and pray about understanding and developing the divine attribute of heavenly peace, please consider the following questions:

- How can you more fully attain the promise of the Lord that peace will come by learning about Him, listening to His words, and walking in the meekness of His Spirit (see D&C 19:23)?

- What confirmation do you find in your own experience that an enduring quality of eternal womanhood is to plant the seeds of peace, nurture relationships of harmony, and help to harvest the fruit of mutual accord and heavenly light?

- How have you been strengthened and encouraged by the examples of honor and devotion in your ancestors' lives?

- What thoughts of hope burn within your soul when you ponder the blessings that will come from joining with your eternal family in the world to come?

- When have you found that the strength of the Lord has helped you to rise above the challenges and tribulations of life and find greater peace?

- Are there opportunities around you to help others find more peace and comfort along the pathway of mortality?

- The scriptures promise that "the Lord will give strength unto his people; the Lord will bless his people with peace" (Psalm 29:11). What are your feelings and experiences relating to this promise?

- How does the blessing of peace engender feelings of gratitude and cheer?

- In what ways do the faithful women in your life rise up as devoted mothers and guardians in Zion?

- In what ways do you find the spirit of eternal womanhood to be the true essence of peace?

THE DIVINE CALLING OF WOMANHOOD is essential to the work and glory of God to "bring to pass the immortality and eternal life of man" (Moses 1:39). Womanhood is the priceless equivalent of love, the full measure of charity, the embodiment of nurture, and the essence of divine grace as expressed in the lives of mothers, wives, sisters, and daughters who have "lived through the ages and worshiped the true and living God" (D&C 138:39).

We can honor and be grateful to all the daughters of destiny who participate with full resolve in God's plan. We can extol the contributions of womanhood as reflected in the lives of exemplary women down through the ages. We can recognize the valor and example of God's faithful daughters who have manifested love and unshakeable righteousness during their mortal experience.

The lessons learned from the lives of such women can touch our hearts and minds and help us rise above our imperfections and seek the high road of goodness in keeping with the example of our Lord and Master. Womanhood in its most noble manifestation is the essence of godhood; it is the demarcation of the pathway to our heavenly home; womanhood is the inspiring confirmation that the eternal destiny of God's children is a reality.

> "Womanhood in its most noble manifestation is the essence of godhood."

Do we place on the pedestal of perfection the women of our acquaintance—whether in the present time or of past years, whether in our own family line or in the pages of the holy scriptures? No, for they, like all of us, are but *seekers* of perfection, who strive to overcome weaknesses and rise in goodness through the strength of the Lord. We can follow in their footsteps as they embrace the counsel of the Lord: "Come, follow me" (Luke 18:22). They can show us through word and deed how to rise step-by-step up the ladder of progression toward a fuller understanding of our divine destiny as sons and daughters of God. They can teach us lessons of how to acquire and improve qualities that bless lives, qualities such as those illustrated in this book: divine majesty, loyal love, abundant sharing, eternal light, noble leadership, gifted life, joyful conversion, attuned allegiance, and heavenly peace.

How might the blessings of the Lord help each of us discover new ways in which these divine gifts can flow more abundantly into our lives? We can hope and pray in faith. We can seek truth with abiding devotion. We can apply the guidance of the Spirit in humility and courage.

And we can kneel to thank our Father in Heaven and His Son for the example and love manifested in the lives of the daughters of destiny. These blessed individuals who partake of the spirit of eternal womanhood awaken within us the comfort of certainty that we can look forward to one day returning together to the rest of the Lord, "which rest is the fulness of his glory" (D&C 84:24).

NOTES TO REFERENCES FROM THE LIVING SCENES

CHAPTER ONE
1. Luke 1:28
2. See Luke 3:23–38, giving the lineage of Jesus, back to David and beyond to Adam.
3. Luke 1:30–33
4. Luke 1:37
5. Luke 1:38
6. Isaiah 9:6
7. Luke 1:46–47
8. Luke 1:48–50
9. Alma 24:17–24
10. See Alma 53:17.
11. See Alma 56:46.
12. See Alma 53:13.
13. See Alma 53:14–15; 56:6–8. During the second quarter of the final century BC, Moroni, commander of the Nephite armies, and Helaman, son of Alma, were intensely occupied in defending their land from the violent incursions of the Lamanites. Around 64 BC a particularly acute military situation required reinforcements on the Nephite side. The people of Ammon—Lamanite converts who had been repatriated among the Nephites for safety—were anguished over the tribulations and afflictions of their host Nephites on their behalf and were about to suspend their oath relinquishing forever the use of weapons of war. However, Helaman dissuaded them, fearing that they would thereby imperil their salvation. What could be done to assure victory in the urgent fight against the attacking Lamanites and their turncoat Nephite leaders? Accept the covenant offer of the rising generation, who had made no oath against military campaigns.
14. See Alma 53:21.
15. See Alma 56:47–48.
16. Alma 58:40
17. See Alma 58:40.
18. Alma 56:44
19. Alma 56:45, 47–48

20. Alma 53:20
21. Alma 56:56
22. Alma 57:20–21
23. See Alma 57:6.
24. Alma 57:26–27
25. Alma 58:10
26. Alma 58:11–12
27. From the autobiography of Mary Lightner entitled, "Mary Elizabeth Rollins Lightner," *The Utah Genealogical and Historical Magazine* 17 (July 1926), p. 196; the full article comprises p. 193–205, 250–260; see also the summary accounts included in *Church History in the Fulness of Times*, rev. ed. (Salt Lake City: The Church of Jesus Christ of Latter-day Saints, 1993), p. 132–134; and *Our Heritage* (Salt Lake City: The Church of Jesus Christ of Latter-day Saints, 1993), p. 41.
28. See page 195 of the autobiography of Mary Lightner.
29. Ibid., see p. 194.
30. Ibid., p. 193
31. Ibid., p. 194
32. Ibid., p. 195
33. Ibid., see p. 196.
34. Containing sections 1–65 of the Doctrine and Covenants
35. Ibid., see p. 196.
36. Ibid. p. 199
37. D&C 20:16; this section was included in the original Book of Commandments.

CHAPTER TWO
38. See Ruth 1:4.
39. See Ruth 1:1, 3.
40. Ruth 1:8
41. Ruth 1:9
42. See Ruth 1:9.
43. Ruth 1:10
44. See Ruth 1:14.
45. Ruth 1:16–17
46. See Ruth 2:9.
47. See Ruth 2:14.
48. Ruth 2:12
49. See Ruth 2:15–16.
50. Ruth 2:20
51. See Ruth 2:10.
52. See Ruth 1:16.
53. Ruth 3:11
54. See Ruth 4:17.
55. See Ruth 4:17–22.

56. Sychar, a town in Samaria not far from Mount Ebal and Mount Gerizim; Sychar is also identified with Shechem, one of the chief cities of Northern Israel.

57. See Genesis 33:19 concerning the parcel of ground purchased by Jacob from the sons of Hamor. Jacob built an altar there and apparently also dug a deep well nearby that became known traditionally as Jacob's well.

58. Mount Gerizim, some 2,850 feet above sea level and around 800 feet above the valley floor. Following the return from Babylonian captivity, Gerizim became a center of worship for the Samaritan people.

59. The Samaritans were a people who populated Samaria following the Assyrian captivity of the Northern Kingdom of Israel around 721 BC. Samaria, located in the mountainous region of Palestine, had originally been established as a stronghold capital by Omri, king of Israel (see 1 Kings 16:23–24). The Samaritans were, in general, a blending of those Israelites left behind after the scattering by the Assyrians and the gentile colonists placed in that territory by the Assyrian conquerors (see 2 Kings 17:23–24). Generations later, upon the return of Judah from the Babylonian captivity of the sixth century BC, the Samaritans desired to assist in the rebuilding of the temple at Jerusalem—a privilege denied them by the Jewish leaders (Ezra 4:1–3). Angered, the Samaritans turned against Judah with much animosity and later erected a temple of their own on Mount Gerizim. Gerizim became for the Samaritans what Jerusalem was for the Jewish people. Despite the intolerance of the Jewish people (see Matthew 10:5; Luke 9:51–56; Luke 10:33; Luke 17:16; John 4:9, 39; John 8:48), the Samaritans were able, in their time, to receive the gospel message from the disciples of Jesus (see Acts 1:8; Acts 8:4–15).

60. These words and the subsequent excerpts of spoken language in the dialogue are drawn directly from John 4:7–27.

61. This passage comes from JST John 4:26.

62. Jesus showed compassion for the Samaritans on other occasions: see His parable about the Good Samaritan (Luke 10:25–37); the one of the ten lepers healed by the Savior who returned to give thanks was a Samaritan (see Luke 17:16).

63. 1 Corinthians 2:9–10; see also Isaiah 64:4.

CHAPTER THREE

64. 1 Samuel 1:11

65. 1 Samuel 2:19

66. 1 Samuel 1:27–28

67. 1 Samuel 2:2

68. 1 Samuel 2:10

69. See Luke 1:59; it was customary in Jewish practice to circumcise the male baby on the eighth day of his life; see Genesis 17:9–12; also JST Genesis 17:11–17.

70. Compare Luke 1:13.

71. Luke 1:41

72. Luke 1:15

73. Luke 1:25

74. Luke 1:37
75. Luke 1:16–17; the angel was Gabriel (see Luke 1:19, 26).
76. Luke 1:14; echoing the words of the angel Gabriel.
77. See Luke 1:58.
78. Luke 1:60
79. Luke 1:61
80. Luke 1:63
81. Luke 1:64
82. Luke 1:76–79. In addition, we know from modern scripture that an angel—perhaps Gabriel—performed a holy setting apart for the babe at this time: "For he . . . was ordained by the angel of God at the time he was eight days old unto this power, to overthrow the kingdom of the Jews, and to make straight the way of the Lord before the face of his people, to prepare them for the coming of the Lord, in whose hand is given all power" (D&C 84:28; see also D&C 128:21 for a reference to the appearance of Gabriel in the latter days).
83. Malachi 3:10
84. D&C 97:8

CHAPTER FOUR
85. Moses 6:9
86. Moses 4:26; Genesis 3:20
87. Moses 5:11
88. See Moses 5:1.
89. Moses 5:5
90. Moses 5:7
91. Genesis 3:16; Moses 4:22
92. Moses 5:12
93. 1 Samuel 25:24
94. 1 Samuel 25:28
95. 1 Samuel 25:29
96. 1 Samuel 25:30
97. 1 Samuel 25:31
98. 1 Samuel 25:32–33
99. D&C 88:118
100. 2 Nephi 31:20
101. D&C 59:23

CHAPTER FIVE
102. Esther 4:14
103. Esther 4:16
104. Esther 4:11
105. See Esther 2:15, 17.
106. See Esther chapters 5–8.

107. Esther 8:16. The book of Esther presents the historical context and the religious/moral foundation for the establishment of the Jewish feast of Purim. *Purim* is the Hebrew word for "lots"—a reference to the plan of Haman, chief officer at the court of the king of Persia (Ahasuerus, most likely Xerxes, whose rule began around 486 BC), to cast lots for determining a good omen for the timing of his plan for putting all the Jews of the captivity to death (see Esther 3:7; 9:24).

108. See Judges 4:4.

109. See Judges 5:7.

110. See Judges 4:3, 6.

111. Judges 4:7

112. Judges 4:8

113. Judges 4:9

114. Judges 4:14

115. See Judges 4:15–21. It was Jael, wife of Heber the Kenite, a descendant of Jethro, father-in-law of Moses, who took in the fleeing Sisera and soon brought his life to an end.

116. Judges 5:2–3

117. Judges 5:7

118. Judges 5:11–12

119. Judges 5:20

120. Judges 5:31

121. A song written by Ron Harris.

CHAPTER SIX

122. See Genesis 35:10; see also the earlier reference in 32:28.

123. Genesis 17:4

124. See Genesis 30:22–24.

125. See Genesis 31:3, 13; 32:9.

126. See Genesis 31:44, 52–55.

127. See Genesis 33:1–16.

128. See Genesis 35:18.

129. Genesis 30:24

130. See Genesis 35:18.

131. Genesis 29:20

132. Genesis 29:17

133. Luke 10:39

134. John 11:2

135. Luke 10:42

136. John 11:24; these words, spoken by Martha to the Master, were likely shared by Martha with her sister, Mary.

137. John 11:28

138. See John 11:29.

139. John 11:32

140. See John 11:35.
141. John 11:36
142. John 11:40
143. John 11:41–42
144. Luke 10:42
145. John 12:3; see also the references in Matthew 26:6 and Mark 14:3, which indicate that the gathering was at the home of Simon the leper.
146. John 12:7–8
147. John 11:25–26
148. Genesis 3:20 and Moses 4:26. The story shared is about Amy Leone Allen, mother of the author, Richard J. Allen.

CHAPTER SEVEN
149. See Alma 19:3.
150. Alma 19:4
151. Alma 19:8
152. Alma 19:6; see the account of the conversion of King Lamoni in Alma 18:14–42. These events took place around 90 BC.
153. Alma 19:9
154. Ibid.
155. Alma 19:10
156. Alma 19:12–13
157. See Alma 19:13.
158. See Alma 19:14.
159. See Alma 19:15–36; see also in chapter 8 of this book the account of Abish, the faithful woman who caused the queen to rise from the sleep induced by the Spirit of God.
160. See 1 Nephi 2:4.
161. 1 Nephi 5:2
162. 1 Nephi 5:8
163. 1 Nephi 5:9–13
164. See 1 Nephi 5:7.
165. The account comes from the personal journal of the author's wife, Carol Lynn Allen.
166. Psalm 96:11
167. John 17:19
168. D&C 59:23
169. Ruth 1:16

CHAPTER EIGHT
170. Mary Magdalene was from Magdala, a community located on the western shore of the Sea of Galilee. We first learn of her during the account of the Lord's ministry among the various towns in that area (see Luke 8:1–3).
171. See Luke 8:3.

172. See Matthew 27:55–56; Mark 15:41.
173. See Matthew 27:50–56; Mark 15:39–41; Luke 23:46–56; John 19:25–27.
174. See Matthew 27:61; Mark 15:47; Luke 23:55.
175. See Mark 16:1; Luke 23:56; 24:1.
176. See Matthew 28:1–8; Mark 16:1–8; Luke 24:1–11; John 20:1–2.
177. See John 20:3–11.
178. See John 20:11–13.
179. Matthew 28:6; Mark 16:6
180. John 20:15
181. John 20:16
182. See Alma 19:18–19. When Ammon, the son of Mosiah, brought the gospel message to King Lamoni and his people in the land of Ishmael, the Spirit over-powered all members of the household, with the exception of a Lamanite woman named Abish, who had already been converted to the Lord.
183. See Alma 19:20.
184. See Alma 19:17.
185. See Alma 19:22. Ammon was protected in fulfillment of the promise of the Lord to King Mosiah that his sons would be preserved on their mission to the Lamanites (see Mosiah 28:7).
186. See Alma 19:25–27.
187. See Alma 19:16.
188. Alma 19:29; the conversion of the wife of King Lamoni is described in chapter 7.
189. See Alma 19:31.
190. This scene is adapted from the account contained in "Our Heritage," an address given by historian Nicholas G. Morgan Sr., then president of the National Society of the Sons of Utah Pioneers, before the student body at Brigham Young University on October 27, 1953, p. 5–6.
191. See *Church History in the Fulness of Times*, rev. ed. (Salt Lake City: The Church of Jesus Christ of Latter-day Saints, 1993), p. 410–411.

CHAPTER NINE
192. The event took place in the John Johnson home at Hiram, Ohio, on Saturday, March 24, 1832 (see *HC* 1:261–265).
193. D&C 25:3, 5
194. See D&C 25:11–12.
195. See *HC* 1:264.
196. See *HC* 1:265.
197. See *HC* 7:456–477.
198. *HC* 7:470–471
199. See *HC* 7:471.
200. Ibid.
201. Ibid.

202. D&C 137:5; received on January 21, 1836.
203. A shorter version of this account was included in the book *The Art of Motherhood* (American Fork: Covenant Communications, Inc., 2013), p. 93–94. The account comes from the personal journal of the author, Richard J. Allen.
204. Alma 32:41
205. See D&C 138:12–17, 51.

INDEX

ABOUT THE AUTHOR

RICHARD J. ALLEN IS A husband, father, great-grandfather, teacher, and writer. He has served on several high councils, in several stake presidencies, and as a bishop. Richard's teaching assignments in the Church have included service as a full-time missionary, instructor in various priesthood quorums, and Gospel Doctrine teacher for adults and youth. He and his wife, Carol Lynn, have served together as stake institute instructors and stake missionary preparation instructors. Richard has a PhD from The Johns Hopkins University, where he served on the faculty and in the senior administration for a number of years. He was also a faculty member at Brigham Young University. He has served on a number of national educational boards and has authored and coauthored many articles, manuals, and books—including over thirty books with Covenant Communications. He and his wife have four children, five grandchildren, and one great-grandchild.